MW01089400

LAST TO JOIN THE FIGHT

LAST
TO JOIN
THE
FIGHT

THE 66TH GEORGIA INFANTRY

DANIEL CONE

MERCER UNIVERSITY PRESS • MACON, GEORGIA

MERCER
UNIVERSITY PRESS

Endowed by
TOM WATSON BROWN
and
THE WATSON-BROWN FOUNDATION, INC.

MUP/ H882

Published by Mercer University Press, Macon, Georgia 31207
© 2014 by Mercer University Press
1400 Coleman Avenue
Macon, Georgia 31207

All rights reserved

9 8 7 6 5 4 3 2 1

Books published by Mercer University Press are printed on acid-free paper
that meets the requirements of the American National Standard for
Information Sciences—Permanence of Paper for Printed Library Materials.

Library of Congress Cataloging-in-Publication Data

Cone, Daniel, 1977-
  Last to join the fight : the Sixty-Sixth Georgia Infantry / Daniel Cone.
    pages cm
  Includes bibliographical references and index.
  ISBN 978-0-88146-475-7 (hardback : alk. paper) -- ISBN 0-88146-475-9
(hardback : alk. paper)
  1. Confederate States of America. Army. Georgia Infantry Regiment, 66th.
  2. United States--History--Civil War, 1861-1865--Regimental histories.
  3. Georgia--History--Civil War, 1861-1865--Regimental histories. 4. United
States--History--Civil War, 1861-1865--Campaigns. 5. Soldiers--Georgia--
History--19th century. I. Title. II. Title: Sixty-Sixth Georgia Infantry.
  E559.566th .C66 2014
  973.7'458--dc23
                                                    2014002537

Contents

Preface

Hundreds of military units fought in the American Civil War. A large number have been the subject of regimental histories, produced by the war's veterans or veterans' friends, or, in the present day, by veterans' descendants, professional scholars, or amateur buffs. In terms of length, regimental histories vary from a few dozen pages to several hundred. In content, they run the gamut from windy verbosities on the minutiae of military life, to limpid regurgitations of easily-obtainable facts, to noisy polemical screeds, to carefully-considered analyses of what made this or that regiment tick.

Surveying this extensive subgenre of Civil War writing, one might be forgiven for asking, "Why do we need another regimental history?" My answer is that the 66th Georgia Infantry was raised in the late-war period, served entirely in the Western Theater, and fought in the Army of Tennessee. There are too few regimental histories that deal with any one of these factors, much less all three. In spite of an abundance of studies about early-war units from the Eastern Theater, particularly regiments from the Army of Northern Virginia, we have more questions than answers at the regimental level. There is, therefore, still a need to enumerate the subtle but significant differences between the "boys of '61" and the "men of '63," and between Robert E. Lee's often-conquering soldiers in gray, and the brown-and butternut-clad "web-feet" who suffered constant frustrations in the campaigns west of the Appalachians. One book, of course, cannot rectify the imbalance, but it can at least point the way for others.

A few disclaimers are in order. First, I freely admit that my work bears certain similarities to John D. Fowler's *Mountaineers in*

Gray and Edward J. Haggerty's *Collis' Zouaves.*[1] In addition to offering the traditional structure for works in this subgenre—a narrative of the regiment's beginnings, its marches, and its battles—I have assessed demographic data of the rank and file. Crunching numbers in the name of history is no easy thing to do (particularly for a writer with no love of mathematics), nor is it everyone's cup of tea to read the results. Those who prefer to keep their military history free of cliometrics would do well to skip ahead upon seeing paragraphs full of numbers. Second, this book is not intended as a genealogical reference work. Readers who want to know if an ancestor served in the 66th Georgia are encouraged to consult Volume VI of Lillian Henderson's *Roster of the Confederate Soldiers of Georgia* for a full roster of the regiment.[2]

---

[1]John D. Fowler, *Mountaineers in Gray: The Nineteenth Tennessee Volunteer Infantry, C.S.A.* (Knoxville: University of Tennessee Press, 2004); Edward J. Haggerty, *Collis' Zouaves: The 114th Pennsylvania Volunteers in the Civil War* (Baton Rouge: Louisiana State University Press, 1997).

[2]Lillian Henderson, ed., *Roster of the Confederate Soldiers of Georgia, 1861-1865* (Hapeville, GA: Longino & Porter, 1964), Vol VI, 693-771.

Acknowledgments

This book began as a master's thesis for the Public History program at the University of West Georgia. For the research and direction that went into its initial iteration, I would like to thank my thesis committee members, Keith Bohannon (head), Keith Hebert, and Ann McCleary. Each had an important role in shaping the work: Dr. Bohannon generously provided all of his own available materials on the 66th Georgia Infantry and told me where to find more; Dr. Hebert critiqued an initial version of the regimental sample and suggested some crucial adjustments to my methodology; and Dr. McCleary, posed several pointed questions that encouraged me to drill my analysis down a bit deeper. I would also like to thank the staffs at the Georgia Department of Archives and History (GDAH), the Keenan Research Center at the Atlanta History Center (AHC), and the National Archives and Records Administration (NARA).

For the editing necessary to turn a long-winded thesis into a readable book, the credit belongs to Scot Danforth at the University of Tennessee Press, and to my aunt, Ellen Hanson. Though Scot and I did not end up working together on this project, I appreciate all of his assistance with getting it ready for publication. As for Aunt Ellen, she has been my no-nonsense editor-in-chief *par excellence* for many years, on call whenever needed. Whether dealing with capitalization, clarity, or context, there is nothing that her keen eyes have ever missed. Thus, any remaining errors are my own.

Finally, I would like to thank Marc Jolley, Director at Mercer University Press, for taking a chance, in the midst of rather challenging times for the publishing world, on my manuscript.

Colonel James Cooper Nisbet

Source: *Four Years on the Firing Line* (Chattanooga, TN: Imperial Press, 1911)

Lieutenant Colonel Algernon S. Hamilton

Source: *History of The Doles-Cook Brigade, Army of Northern Virginia, C.S.A.*
(Atlanta: Franklin Printing & Publishing Co., 1903)

Adjutant William L. LeConte

Source: "Events of My Life" (N.p., private collection)

Lieutenant Briggs H. Napier, after the war

Source: "Biography of Captain Briggs H. Napier," www.armoryguards.org

Sergeant John M. Davis and his wife, after the war

Source: "John Morgan Davis – Family Tree," hawkofgeorgia.com

Captain Moses L. Brown

Courtesy of the David Wynn Vaughan Collection

Assistant Quartermaster Cecil C. Hammock

Courtesy of the David Wynn Vaughan Collection

Sergeant George W. Musick

Source: Wiggins, Dr. David R., *Remembering Georgia's Confederates*; Charleston, SC, Chicago, IL, Portsmouth, NH, and San Francisco, CA: Altamira Press, 2005

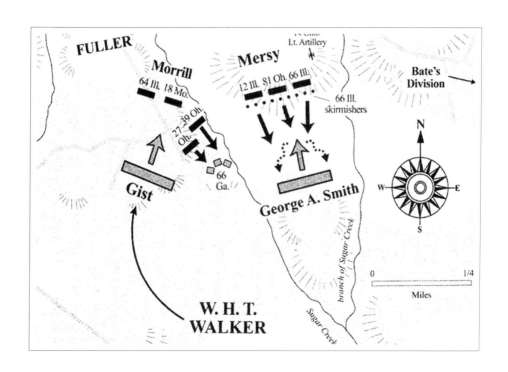

The Sixty-Sixth Georgia at Atlanta, July 22, 1864

Source: Ecelbarger, Gary, *The Day Dixie Died: The Battle of Atlanta*;
New York: Thomas Dunne Books, 2010

James Cooper Nisbet, after the war

Source: "Find A Grave – Col James Cooper Nisbet," www.findagrave.com

Introduction

On a sultry July day 150 years ago, a young officer sat down in the red Georgia clay to write a letter to his mother. Just shy of twenty years old, he had been a soldier for three years, first as a private in the ranks, and now as a lieutenant leading a company of men. Until a few days prior, he had never experienced combat, and indeed had confessed that he was ready to shirk everything except honor to stay out of harm's way. No doubt, he looked over at his sword and haversack, both recently clipped by enemy bullets. "It is really strange that I got out safe," he told his mother, "for I never saw [musket] balls come thicker in my life." After describing some of what he had seen, the officer closed "I will write again soon."[1]

William Redding Ross did write home again, but his loved ones—who would receive his next, and final, letter in a heartbreaking way—soon learned that whatever had protected the Confederate lieutenant at the battles of Peach Tree Creek and Atlanta had not protected him to the end of the Civil War. Along with hundreds of soldiers in the 66th Georgia Infantry Regiment, Ross became a blood sacrifice to a doomed cause. Drawn, willingly or not, into the ranks of one of the last units raised for the Confederate States Army, Ross and many of his men gave their youth, their health, and their lives, in defense of their home state. In spite of all the blood they spilled, there was little honor accrued to them, and what they had done soon passed from the memories of many of their fellow soldiers.

Unlike other Confederate units, the 66th Georgia Infantry never achieved any particular service distinction. With the

---

[1] "Battlefield Letters to Mother and Sweetheart," *Atlanta Journal*, 25 April 1943, 8–9.

exception of the commander, Colonel James Cooper Nisbet, whose *Four Years on the Firing Line* (1911) remains one of the classic Confederate memoirs, there is little about the regiment that is familiar to Civil War scholars.[2] Not withstanding its relative obscurity, the 66th Georgia merits a closer look. What kinds of men waited until 1863 to serve in the 66th and other units of the Confederate Army, and what were the prewar backgrounds of men who were, at least in part, conscripted? And, how well did late-war regiments fight?

Most existing studies of Civil War soldiers and the units in which they served focus on the earliest volunteers. As Kenneth Noe has noted in *Reluctant Rebels* (2010), too many historians have lumped all Civil War soldiers into "one military melting pot…in spite of when they enlisted," with the result that "the voices of the earliest and most ardent dominate."[3] When these first volunteers died off from battle or disease, their places were taken by other recruits who, though they had often been eligible for service earlier, had resisted joining up. Why did so many men on both sides wait until 1862 or later to join? Were they shrewdly expecting to collect large bonuses, confident that their services would not be needed, or unwilling to fight until compelled? Noe addressed later-enlisting Confederate soldiers as a whole in *Reluctant Rebels*, and suggested that they were motivated more by a desire to protect their homes than by any states' rights, pro-slavery, or anti-Yankee ideology.[4]

Did these late-war soldiers fight well in combat, or did they desert in droves? According to Noe, later-enlisting Confederates

---

[2] James C. Nisbet, *Four Years on the Firing Line* (Chattanooga TN: Imperial Press, 1911).

[3] Kenneth W. Noe, *Reluctant Rebels: The Confederates who Joined the Army after 1861* (Chapel Hill: University of North Carolina Press, 2010) 6–7.

[4] Noe, *Reluctant Rebels,* 36–37, 60, 102.

generally gave a good account of themselves, even though their older average ages and poorer health sometimes kept them out of combat altogether. Furthermore, later-enlisting Confederates, though often grumblers, stayed in the war until the bitter end.[5] The men of the 66th Georgia generally fit Noe's description.

Assembled in the middle of the Civil War, the 66th Georgia Infantry Regiment was a mixture of volunteers, conscripts, and substitutes, drawn from many different counties. Its social makeup reflected the society from which it was formed: most of the men in the ranks were farmers, many were destitute, and only a small percentage owned slaves. Apart from Colonel Nisbet, very few of the regiment's officers had any military experience. Due perhaps to unproven leadership, the 66th Georgia suffered heavy attrition in its first year of service. Having become depleted, the regiment fared poorly in battle. The postwar years were not kind to the memory of the 66th Georgia. Its veterans showed little interest in remembering their wartime experiences, and other Confederates forgot that the regiment had existed at all. Their story deserves to be told. The men of the 66th Georgia, like other Civil War soldiers, were both brave and cowardly, dutiful and shirking. Though the first Confederate volunteers later derided the services of late-war soldiers, the majority of the 66th stuck it out through trying times and fought as hard as they could under the circumstances. This book looks at who these men were, what they did, and how they have been since been regarded (or misunderstood).

---

[5] Noe, *Reluctant Rebels,* 190, 195, 198, 206.

Chapter 1

The Birth Place of the Regiment: Georgia in 1863

"A New Regiment for the Department of Middle-Florida," proclaimed a short advertisement in the *Milledgeville Confederate Union* in spring 1863. In the lower corner of the newspaper's second page, the advertisement informed Georgians that another military unit was being raised for the Confederate Army. The regiment's commander would gladly accept into his ranks "Companies of sixty-four, squads, non-conscripts or exempts… residing in…the following named counties: Baker, Calhoun, Clay, Decatur, Dougherty, Early, Lee, Mitchell, Miller, Randolph, Terrell, Thomas, Worth, Chattahoochee, Marion, Quitman, Stewart, Sumter, Schley, Taylor, Webster, Muscogee…"

Reading the advertisement, young, able-bodied men in Milledgeville might have noted that their county, Baldwin, was absent from the list. For them, the next few lines—"Also non-conscripts, exempts, and those subject to conscription"—would have been a reminder that Georgia relied in part on compulsory service to fill the ranks of the Confederate Army. This was the stick of Confederate military policy, which the advertisement balanced with a few, choice carrots. Volunteers would receive "a bounty of $50 and a complete outfit," and the regiment would be "thoroughly equipped" and "armed with Enfield rifles," the best weapons available to Confederate soldiers. Finally, a separate, shorter notice addressed potential recruits who wanted to serve but dreaded the thought of leaving their families. "The Regiment will be assigned to duty in Southern Georgia," it reassured them, "affording those who join…an opportunity to go into service near home."[1]

Five months later, more than 1,200 men in grey and butternut uniforms marched off to serve for a year and a half in this new regiment. They traveled from instruction camps in Middle Georgia to garrison camps in Florida, and fought from the heights near Chattanooga to the rolling countryside near Atlanta. The men of the 66th Georgia Infantry witnessed the waning of Southern hopes for victory, the decline and defeat of the Confederate Army, and the destruction of the Confederate nation. They suffered from heat and cold, hunger, illness, hideous wounds, and death in overcrowded hospitals and furious battles. Some lost faith in the Confederate cause and deserted the regiment; others persevered to the end. A mere handful survived to return to a devastated Georgia, the home that they had been told they would not have to leave.

When the above advertisement first appeared, the Civil War was almost two years old—"a mere infant," noted the *Macon Daily Telegraph*, "yet…a hoary reprobate." Few Georgians had anticipated that the war would have lasted so long; fewer still had expected that it would become all-consuming. "War," the *Telegraph* decided in March 1863, "now appears to be the normal condition and regular pursuit of the human race." Taking stock of the situation, the paper proclaimed that, though the war would go on for some time, "we still hope to outlive the contest."[2]

Guarded optimism characterized the tone of other major Georgia newspapers during this period. Though "the time is not yet come for [the North] to give up the contest," one Augusta newspaper was certain "we shall beat the Yankees, we believe."

[1] *Milledgeville Confederate Union*, 24 March 1863.
[2] *Macon Daily Telegraph,* 14 March 1863.

Another Augusta paper declared that Georgia's citizens "have every reason to be hopeful, confident of final success," despite the great odds against them. A few days later, the same paper described the war situation as "full of interest, and not devoid of danger," but yet "not alarming, [or] extremely serious."[3] Georgia had a hard road to travel before the coming of peace, but the state's press was sure she would arrive safely.

An impartial observer reading these pronouncements might see little more than wishful thinking, for by the beginning of 1863, the Confederacy faced daunting odds. More than one million Federal soldiers confronted half that number of Confederates, and while the North could call upon tens of thousands more men if necessary, the South could not. The powerful United States Navy was slowly strangling the South by blockading and seizing Southern ports. Not only was the Confederacy outnumbered and isolated, it was also steadily losing ground. Two-thirds of Tennessee, half of Arkansas, and sizeable swaths of Alabama, Louisiana, Mississippi, and the Carolina coasts were in Northern hands. Gone with that territory were precious resources of food, industry, materiel, and manpower, all necessary to the Confederacy's war-making efforts.

Georgia was in a somewhat better situation than many of her Confederate sister states. Very little Georgia territory was under Northern occupation, and though it was suffering from the blockade, the state maintained a modest trade with the outside world. Still, Federal amphibious forces had seized and garrisoned many of Georgia's coastal islands in 1862, and threatened Savannah, the state's largest city. When the Federal navy probed Fort McAllister, one of Savannah's protective forts, early that March, it seemed initially that the city might fall. Northern

---

[3] *Augusta Chronicle*, 3 March 1863; *Augusta Daily Constitutionalist*, 20 and 24 March 1863.

ironclad monitors fired "fifty to sixty tons of iron ball" at the fort, during a long bombardment.[4] Thankfully for the Confederate defenders, the fort withstood the barrage and the monitors withdrew, but the Federal navy could always try again.

Despite the dangers, Georgia's Confederates had good reason to expect ultimate Southern victory during the third spring of the war. After all, their national armies were riding high on a wave of recent battlefield successes. In Virginia, General Robert E. Lee's Army of Northern Virginia had inflicted a bloody repulse on the Federal Army of the Potomac at Fredericksburg (13 December 1862). On the banks of the Mississippi River, Confederate forces under General John C. Pemberton had consistently frustrated Federal attempts to capture Vicksburg, Mississippi, and Port Hudson, Louisiana, which defended the river valley. In central Tennessee, a costly engagement at Murfreesboro (31 December 1862–2 January 1863) had temporarily halted the advance of the Federal Army of the Cumberland towards Chattanooga, the northern gateway to Georgia. Added to a string of Confederate successes the previous summer and fall, these battles showed that the Confederacy was still full of fight.

Georgians also believed that the North was growing weary of the fighting and might be willing to negotiate peace. Some Northerners had never supported the war at all, while others were dispirited by successive Northern defeats, severe Northern casualties, and no clear sign of victory. Thousands of officers and men in the Union Army were said to be deserting because of exhaustion, hatred of army life, or homesickness. Rumors were rife about an imminent national draft that would force half-hearted Northerners into the army against their will. Strikes, sabotage, and anti-war riots broke out that spring in the Pennsylvania

---

[4] *Augusta Chronicle,* 7 March 1863.

backcountry and parts of the Midwest. Could the North overcome the South while fighting a fire in its rear as well?

To win the war, Georgia's Confederates would have to give their all against considerable odds. Because the North would probably add another "three millions of men" to the field before the end of the year, the *Milledgeville Confederate Union* urged the Confederate Congress to increase the size of the armies and compel the obedience of the people. "Let those who are able to fight, go the field," it urged, "and those who stay at home make bread and meat for those who are fighting." An Augusta paper expected Union General Ulysses S. Grant to renew his attempts to take Vicksburg, and pointed out that, "while the Mississippi remains in our power the Confederacy is unconquerable." The *Atlanta Southern Confederacy* agreed; a victory in the Western Theater, especially in the Mississippi River Valley, was absolutely critical.[5]

While most Georgia newspapers were awed by Northern military power, a few were contemptuous of it. Federal soldiers, though great in number, were considered inferior to Confederate soldiers as fighting men. "Let [the North] drag her unwilling conscripts to the field," boasted the *Macon Daily Telegraph*, "She may perhaps gather *more* men, but the morale will be lacking." What difference had been made by the multitude of Northern soldiers who enlisted in 1862? "Fredericksburg, Murfreesboro, Vicksburg…and Port Hudson full prove that Southern valor is much more than a match for Northern numbers," the same paper declared later that spring. An Augusta newspaper admitted that the Confederacy was badly outnumbered, but felt that

---

[5] *Milledgeville Confederate Union*, 3 March 1863; *Augusta Chronicle*, 18 March 1863; *Atlanta Southern Confederacy*, 25 March 1863.

"[Northern] numbers should inspire no alarm." The Yankees who survived combat would soon die of heat and malaria anyway.[6]

The state press bristled with pugnacity in spring 1863. "We have need to 'gird up our loins,'" the *Atlanta Southern Confederacy* announced, "and fight on—fight ever—until [the North's] myrmidons are expelled from the soil they are polluting." The *Milledgeville Confederate Union* believed victory would come from "hitting the enemy hard blows, and putting them on thick and fast." "Defeat will not subdue us," wrote the *Augusta Daily Constitutionalist*, "but victories will demoralize the enemy." The *Augusta Chronicle* claimed that peace would only come from "the hero's arm, when his sabre flashes...amid the smoke of battle." Most direct of all was a column in the *Athens Southern Banner* entitled "TRUTH IN A NUTSHELL": "Now is the time to fight"; "Our best advocates are...delivered by 'cannon, mortar and petard,'"; "Our only reliance lies in our prowess on the field"; "So long as we whip [the Yankees], they are like...spaniels...and obedient servants"; "Stand there, Confederate soldiers! under your glorious battle flag, and defy all the ends of the earth to haul it down."[7]

If the key to winning was to fight hard, then the keepers of the keys were the Confederacy's main armies. One, the Army of Northern Virginia under General Lee, had won almost every one of its battles, and inspired confidence in Georgia's Confederates. The other, General Braxton Bragg's Army of Tennessee, had fought savagely but without real success in Kentucky and

---

[6] *Macon Daily Telegraph,* 4 and 20 March 1863; *Augusta Daily Constitutionalist,* 20 March 1863.

[7] *Atlanta Southern Confederacy,* March 25, 1863; *Milledgeville Confederate Union,* 3 March 1863; *Augusta Daily Constitutionalist,* 24 March 1863; *Augusta Chronicle,* 15 March 1863; *Athens Southern Banner,* 11 March 1863.

Tennessee.[8] General Pemberton's separate forces in Mississippi and Louisiana were holding their own.

It was the hard-luck Army of Tennessee that elicited the most commentary from Georgia newspapers in the third spring of the war. Bragg's forces were said to be "in a splendid condition in every respect," with "infantry…augmented considerably," and "20,000 of the finest cavalry in the world." A small victory in early March by some of that cavalry, under General Earl Van Dorn, was trumpeted as a "perfect success" that reportedly cost the Federals over 2,500 men. An Augusta editor declared that Bragg was securely positioned; that the opposing Federal army under General William Rosecrans was paralyzed by muddy roads; and that more than 12,000 Federal reinforcements had been derailed by Van Dorn's raids. Touring the Army of Tennessee in mid-March, a correspondent for the *Chattanooga Rebel* found everyone energetic and kept busy in drills. Duly noting admiration in the ranks for some of Bragg's generals, such as Leonidas Polk, William Hardee, and John Breckenridge, the reporter nonetheless thought the army's real heroes were its regimental colonels. "Those noble chiefs of clans," he wrote, "whose knightly valor and strong capacity mould the…troops into pure and warlike immages [sic]…many of them…fit to lead armies [and] control states" were the army's "bone and sinew." With such advantages, the papers had "every confidence in the Army of Tennessee."[9]

---

[8] Not to be confused with the Federal Army of *the* Tennessee, which fought in many of the same campaigns.

[9] *Augusta Daily Constitutionalist,* 11 March 1863; *Augusta Chronicle,* 8 March 1863; *Augusta Daily Constitutionalist,* 17 and 20 March 1863; *Macon Daily Telegraph,* 19 March 1863 (*Chattanooga Rebel* citation).

Some of this confidence was well founded, for the army was generally in good condition and fairly well-led. Left unspoken were genuine concerns about whether Bragg's men could hold middle Tennessee. Supplies were barely trickling in, the position was too thin for an effective defense, and, most alarmingly, a number of Bragg's generals were clamoring for his head.[10] A full disclosure of these difficulties would hardly have boosted the spirits of Georgia families, for any further retreat by Bragg would bring the war right to the northern border of the state.

Some Georgians remained hopeful that future victories by the Army of Tennessee and other Confederate forces would lead to foreign intervention. The *Augusta Chronicle* reported that French Emperor Napoleon III "was lately heard to declare himself converted to the separation in America," and was, according to the same source, anxious for a foreign war in order to thwart his political opponents. A Macon newspaper offered no comparable details about diplomatic developments, but was no less certain of the future: "Recognition of our rights as an independent nation, by European Governments, must come, sooner or later."[11]

Others were not sure that they really wanted foreign recognition. The *Augusta Daily Constitutionalist* carefully contrasted *recognition* with *intervention*, and decided that neither would guarantee Confederate independence. Recognition by England and France, the paper argued, would be nothing more than a legal formality, a toothless, *de jure* admission of the Confederacy's *de facto* nationhood. What would mere recognition accomplish? "It would not involve the United States in a war with either of those powers," and more importantly, "the blockade would not be

---

[10] Steven Woodworth, *Six Armies in Tennessee: The Chickamauga and Chattanooga Campaign* (Lincoln: University of Nebraska Press, 1998) 6–16.

[11] *Augusta Chronicle,* 8 March 1863; *Macon Daily Telegraph,* 20 March 1863.

raised." Intervention, whether "friendly" (i.e., as mediators) or "armed," would also do little good; the former would founder on the inability of the North and the South to come to agreeable terms, while the latter "would impose...the views of European sovereigns...[on] our own government."[12]

Even amongst those Confederates that wanted recognition, there was some doubt that it would actually happen. "England," an Atlanta newspaper griped, "stands aloof in the cold selfishness of her neutrality." Blaming the English for first "having planted slavery amongst us," to make themselves rich, and then becoming virulently anti-slavery, the paper could not understand why England had no sympathy for "men of her own race and lineage— men who speak her language, read her books, [and] copy her laws." The French might prove more pliant allies, "but European complications have come to thwart [France]'s mission of justice and generosity." A Milledgeville editor believed that it was hopeless to look for help overseas. "The Mediation and Intervention humbugs," he wrote, " are played out."[13]

There was also disagreement between Georgia's Confederates about whether sowing dissension on the Northern home front was a worthwhile stratagem. An editor from the *Milledgeville Confederate Union* who believed in winning the war this way was alarmed when a counterpart from Richmond, Virginia, classified all Northerners as the enemy and urged no negotiations with them. "Have we not got enemies enough?" the Milledgeville editor wondered aloud, "Or have we got too many friends and allies already that those who would be our friends and allies are spurned with contempt?" "It seems to us it is good policy to get help from every quarter we can," the editor argued, "and if we cannot make

---

[12] *Augusta Daily Constitutionalist,* 10 March 1863.

[13] *Atlanta Southern Confederacy,* 25 March 1863; *Milledgeville Confederate Union,* 3 March 1863.

active partizans [sic] in our favor…yet there will be much gained if [the Midwest] can be drawn from the support of our enemies."[14]

The *Athens Southern Banner* was unconvinced by such arguments. In early March, the paper reminded its readers that Lincoln had been given considerable power by the Northern Congress, and would use that power to crush peace movements in the Midwest. Divisions between Republicans and Northern Democrats over the conduct of the war were only so much hot air. "[The Republicans] favor the war for the purpose of abolishing slavery," the *Banner* noted, while "the Democrats…favor the war for 'restoring the Union.'" The important fact was, "they both agree to fight us." Thus, the paper concluded, "we have no friends at the North…[and no] help from any quarter, except from our own strong arms and brave hearts."[15]

Two weeks later, the *Banner* elaborated on its arguments against relying on Northern dissent. Northern resistance to the draft would be futile, as most draft dodgers were unarmed. Not a single Northern governor would dare to call for peace—he would instantly be removed from power—or recall his state's troops, who would continue to fight for Lincoln simply because *he* paid them. Some Northerners talked about peace, but, as far as the *Banner* could see, there were none "that want or advocate peace except upon the platform of Reconstruction." Yet the main obstacles thwarting a negotiated peace were the lengths that the North had already gone to in order to win:

> On the part of the Union, every nerve has been strained to present the most formidable front…With appropriations of men and money too sweeping to command belief, [the North] threatens the death-blow… With armies grander than those of

---

[14] *Milledgeville Confederate Union,* 10 March 1863.
[15] *Athens Southern Banner,* 4 March 1863.

Alexander or Napoleon…they propose to march through the land… The North is bent upon our subjugation.— Their leaders…know the fruits that will accrue to them from a conquest of the South… Such are the incentives the enemy have to persevere. What man of spirit will submit?[16]

The North, then, had gone too far to back down without a final, cataclysmic fight. It was up to the South to match blow for blow, relying on nothing more nor less than "our little navy" and "our armies" for victory.[17]

Though events on the war front seemed favorable, there were concerns about how the Southern home front was holding up. Financing the war and feeding the armies were becoming more difficult. Like most states of the lower South, Georgia had plenty of cotton but few foodstuffs. Because so much Southern wealth had been sunk into slavery, there was little liquid capital with which to repair Confederate railroads, buy and repair Confederate weapons, and pay Confederate soldiers.

The simplest solutions would be to reduce cotton planting in favor of corn and wheat, and to implement a wise, balanced tax policy. Georgia newspapers advocated such measures that spring. "Plant Corn," the *Augusta Daily Constitutionalist* advised its readers, and plenty of it. "[Georgia], planted in corn, will yield from five to eight millions of bushels…and…it will all be needed." In consideration of the value of cotton, the Georgia legislature allowed a maximum of three acres on each farm. To some Georgians, even this seemed too much. A Milledgeville paper put the matter plainly: "The man who plants cotton to sell, is as much guilty of stabbing the heart of our country as the meanest Abolitionist in Lincoln's army… Every acre of ground put in

---

[16] *Athens Southern Banner,* 18 March 1863.
[17] Ibid.

cotton…is just so much aid to comfort 'the enemy'". The *Macon Daily Telegraph* felt the same way. "If [the people] desire the blessings of peace and security," they should "plant corn, and everything else necessary for the subsistence of man and beast." As for raising money, the best policy was a flat tax on all property owned per head; such was Georgia's policy, wrote the *Augusta Chronicle,* and it seemed to work.[18]

Proposing such measures was far easier than implementing them. Some Georgians blamed the Confederate Congress for imbalanced fiscal policies that had weakened the country. According to the *Augusta Daily Constitutionalist,* the poor were paying too much, the rich too little, and the government, now more than $500 million in debt, seemed unwilling to fix the tax codes. "Will the Congress delay," the paper asked, "till the country has entirely lost confidence…till everything has advanced fifty-fold, till the poor can no longer buy even the plainest food, till a Colonel's pay will not tend his force, till the soldier's family is starving?" Unless the people, who were "patriotic enough to make sacrifices" and "abundantly able to pay taxes," were assessed according to their means, "demoralization and discontent [will] spread from the cabin hearthstone to the camp." Responding to this article, a Bartow County man voiced his approval: "Make our currency good by taxation, and we whip this fight."[19]

Sufficient food was also a necessity, although Georgia Confederates were by no means united on how to produce it. One Georgia editor attributed the scarcity of provisions to hoarders who kept surplus food and sold it at absurdly high prices. "Thousands of these avaricious men," he wrote, "who have their

---

[18] *Augusta Daily Constitutionalist,* 21 March 1863; *Milledgeville Confederate Union,* 3 March 1863; *Macon Daily Telegraph,* 20 March 1863; *Augusta Chronicle,* 4 March 1863.

[19] *Augusta Daily Constitutionalist,* 6 and 15 March 1863.

barns full of corn, their smokehouses full of meat, and their yards full of poultry, owe a great deal of money." Tax them unmercifully, and "we should hear no more of...starvation." Another editor believed that Georgia should build canals and clear naval obstructions on the Savannah River, which would increase intrastate trade. The most common targets of complaint were Georgia planters. "What are [they] doing towards planting their spring crops?" wondered the *Augusta Chronicle*, "Is all the available force about the plantation at work? We hope so. Bread for the army and the people at home must be had."[20]

Confederate authorities usually obtained extra food by impressment, in which purchasing agents forcibly took surplus food or other products in exchange for a government-determined value. Due to high inflation rates in the Confederacy—which reached more than 1,000 percent of 1860 values by the end of the war—and all-too-common abuses by the agents, the practice usually left farmers and other producers destitute, and provoked howls of protest. "If [the people] have property taken" at a low value, the *Augusta Daily Constitutionalist* argued, "they come to lose proper regard...for the government, and will slacken their efforts to produce abundant supplies." Another Augusta paper listed the evil fruits of impressment. Trade had ceased, for fear of confiscation at the market; farmers were planting non-edible crops; food prices were rising at an astronomical rate; and, consequently, Confederate soldiers starved in a land of relative plenty. Some citizens of the Confederacy even threatened violence against impressment agents. "[Impressment] is a foolish idea," the *Constitutionalist* decided, that "stimulates fraud, deters cultivation

---

[20] *Augusta Chronicle,* 17, 25, and 31 March 1863.

of food crops, and threatens the land with famine." It should only be used under dire circumstances.[21]

Georgia's civilians were exhorted to endure the scarcities and sacrifices of the war in order to sustain the state's soldiery. Ninety thousand Georgians—almost one-tenth of the state's pre-war population—were at the front, serving in the Confederate Army. Only their efforts could ensure the safety of the state and its people. Georgia's early troop mobilizations had a noticeable ardor. In the first six months of the war (April–October 1861), Georgia's native sons had joined thirty-six Confederate infantry regiments, two infantry battalions, six batteries of artillery, and two legions.[22] Fueled variously by patriotism, peer pressure, state pride, hatred of Yankees, and eagerness to escape parental control while impressing young ladies, the "boys of '61" willingly went off to war expecting a quick Southern victory and a triumphal return as conquering heroes.

It was not long before the eager young volunteers had learned that war follows its own timetable. Drill, organization, and the monotonous routines of camp life had consumed most days, and the Confederacy's leaders had not undertaken the "lightning war" that their men had envisioned. Though some Georgians had seen early action in western Virginia and at First Manassas (21 July 1861), most had spent their first campaign season marching and countermarching, never coming to blows with the enemy.

Even after it had become clear that the war would not be won before Christmas, as so many had expected, Georgia had not had

---

[21] *Augusta Daily Constitutionalist,* 8 and 24 March 1863; *Augusta Chronicle,* 15 March 1863.

[22] Joseph H. Crute, Jr., *Units of the Confederate Army* (Midlothian VA: Derwent Books, 1987) 80–127. Legions were made up of infantry, cavalry, and artillery elements. Though quite popular in the early-war period, they were soon discontinued and their components distributed amongst the separate branches of service.

great difficulty recruiting additional soldiers. Between November 1861, and February 1862, volunteers from the state had formed another ten infantry regiments, two infantry battalions, two each of cavalry regiments and battalions, and three artillery batteries. Most of these new units had served on the Georgia and Carolina coasts.[23]

Notwithstanding the early recruiting pace, Georgia's Confederates had expressed concern about the future. Newspapers had reported that plenty of able-bodied young men were lounging around at home or on the streets, showing little inclination to join the Confederate Army. Displeased with Georgians' waning enthusiasm, state and Confederate leaders had threatened to use the draft if additional recruits did not come forward.

Confederate President Jefferson Davis had long wrestled with the problem of insufficient manpower. Believing that the war would last a long time, and that the short-term enlistments of 1861 had been a mistake, he had tried to boost the Confederate Army's limited numbers by enticing soldiers to stay on duty longer. The Furlough and Bounty Act of December 1861 had given Confederate soldiers who reenlisted a $50 bounty, a sixty-day furlough to visit home, and the opportunity to elect new officers and reorganize their companies. Further acts in January and February 1862 had provided additional bounties, and allowed the president to accept individual recruits and appoint field officers to raise new units. Unfortunately for Davis, early-war Confederate victories at Manassas and Leesburg, Virginia, and at Wilson's Creek and Lexington, Missouri, had led many Southerners to believe that the war would soon be over. Also, most

---

[23] Crute, Jr., *Units of the Confederate Army*, 80–127.

Confederates in service were farmers, and despite the promised bounties many had left the army for the harvest season.[24]

The year 1862 had opened with Confederate defeats in Arkansas, Tennessee, and the Carolinas. In no small part, these defeats had owed to the Confederacy's depleted forces. Even more frightening had been the possibility that the few men still at the front would go home when their twelve-month enlistments expired. With Federal forces poised to march into the Deep South and against the capital at Richmond, Virginia, the Confederate Congress had passed, and Davis had signed, the First Conscription Act of April 1862. All men in the army would remain in service for another three years, or until the war ended. In addition, all able-bodied white males between the ages of eighteen and thirty-five were required to serve, except for those in certain exempted occupations (such as Confederate and state officials, mail carriers, railroad employees, and teachers). Though very few men had been drafted initially, the Conscription Act had boosted volunteering, as many previously-reluctant men had joined up in order to avoid this stigma.[25]

Conscription in Georgia had given a much-needed shot in the arm to Confederate manpower. Thirty-three new units from the state had joined the Confederate Army between April and December 1862. Less than half of the new levies were infantry units, in contrast to the previous levies, where they had made up three-fourths. Alongside fifteen new infantry regiments, there were four new cavalry units, ten new artillery units, two new battalions of partisan rangers, and two new battalions of sharpshooters.[26]

---

[24] Albert Burton Moore, *Conscription and Conflict in the Confederacy* (New York: Macmillan Co., 1924) 6–10, 52–53.

[25] Ibid., 12–15.

[26] Crute, Jr., *Units of the Confederate Army*, 80–127.

Plenty of Southerners had groused about compulsory military service, but comparatively few had actively resisted it. Many men already in service had approved of the new act because it forced others to do their share in defense of the Confederacy. Still, according to the only national study of Confederate conscription, "it is a safe assumption that conscription could not have been adopted by a popular referendum."[27] Conscription clashed with Southern individualism, garnered opposition from Confederate politicians and jurists, and fomented brutal and bloody little rebellions in several parts of the Confederacy.[28]

Though the state's newspapers made little mention of it at the time, many Georgians were quite angry about being forced to leave their families and serve in the army. What made the situation worse was a well-founded popular perception that the draft penalized the poor. Conscription exempted those who owned twenty or more slaves, and others who could pay for a substitute to take their place might never have to enter the army either. Men of means frequently bribed conscription officers and court justices to avoid going into the army, leaving poorer men to shoulder the burden. In this way, the "economic and political realities [of conscription]…worked against the plain folk," who made their anger clear. At one enrollment of conscripts at Savannah in April 1862, not a single man had appeared, while in the northeast, "over half the soldiers…had 'skedaddled' and were hiding out in the mountains."[29]

Among the opponents of conscription, few were as formidable as Georgia's wartime governor, Joseph Brown. A staunch advocate

---

[27] Ibid., 17.

[28] Ibid., 17–26, 118–20, 148–49.

[29] David Williams, Teresa Crisp Williams, and David Carlson, *Plain Folk in a Rich Man's War: Class and Dissent in Confederate Georgia* (Gainesville: University of Florida Press, 2002) 92–107, 113–30.

of states' rights, Brown had believed that giving the Confederate government power to determine military service would destroy Georgia's political autonomy. Furthermore, Brown had pointed out, Confederate volunteers had kept winning victories (at least, in Virginia); why, therefore, did the army need conscripts? Because Georgia ranked fourth in state contributions to Confederate military service, Brown's protests were dangerous, but under immediate pressure, Brown had acquiesced to the practice of compulsory service, though he had continued to object to the principle.[30]

The Confederate government had continued to refine conscription as the war progressed. A Second Conscription Act, passed in September 1862, had made older men eligible for service, while exempting overseers, millers, tanners, shipbuilders, and other occupations necessary to the war effort. "The most lamented feature of the conscription system," according to historian Albert Moore, was substitution. Intended to relieve men from the army for home-front production, substitution had ended up creating a mess. Prices for substitutes ranged from $1,500 to $3,000 per man, creating a class of mercenaries called "bounty-jumpers," who took the places of drafted men, then left the army once they had received the money. All too often only wealthy men could afford substitutes. Bowing to popular condemnation, the Confederate Congress finally ended substitution in December 1863.[31]

---

[30] Joseph Howard Parks, *Joseph E. Brown of Georgia* (Baton Rouge: Louisiana State University Press, 1976) 198–212; Moore, *Conscription and Conflict,* 255–79. Only Virginia, Tennessee, and North Carolina supplied more troops to the Confederate army.

[31] Moore, *Conscription and Conflict,* 27–51.

The temporary boost provided by conscription had faded by the end of 1862.[32] True, fifteen units were created in Georgia the next year—but ten of these were merely reorganizations of, or consolidations with, existing units. Only two new Georgia infantry regiments were recruited from scratch for the Confederate Army in 1863. One was the 64th, which had started gathering men over the winter, but did not complete its organization until the following spring; the other was the 66th.[33] They would be the last.

Whether volunteers or conscripts, Georgia's soldiers received encouragement from the home front, coupled with warnings against failure. Georgia Confederates knew that their native sons in the army needed supplies, and that soldiers' families needed care as well. A number of benevolent associations had formed to take care of soldier families, and scores of women's groups assembled to make other necessities for the men at the front. Ira Foster, the state's quartermaster general, reported with pride at the beginning of March that the ladies of Georgia had produced "coats, pants, shirts, drawers, shoes, and hats, together with several thousand pairs of socks," for seven Georgia regiments in the Army of Northern Virginia. Another association in Atlanta, formed in mid-March, raised almost $12,000 in pledges within three days.[34] Gifts like these eased some of the burdens on Georgia soldiers and their families.

---

[32] Incomplete records show that up to 300,000 men may have been added to Confederate forces "east of the Mississippi" by conscription. Georgia had at least 8,993 men conscripted during the war, compared with 15,346 exempted (Ibid., 107, 356–57).

[33] The 65th Georgia Infantry, which completed its regimental organization at the same time as the 64th, was filled out from an existing infantry battalion (Crute, Jr., *Units of the Confederate Army*, 116–17).

[34] *Augusta Chronicle*, 1 March 1863; *Macon Daily Telegraph*, 16 March 1863.

Should they falter in their duties, Georgia's Confederate soldiers had a frightening image of what might happen to their families. Reporting on an anti-Confederate uprising in eastern Tennessee, the *Athens Southern Banner* found that Confederate families had been viciously targeted. "The [rioters] are burning and destroying houses," the paper reported, "razing fences, stealing horses, shooting cattle and hauling off all the provisions… Citizens are robbed of their money, and their houses pillaged." Even worse, "three…fair, modest, virtuous young women [were] ruthlessly violated." Though the article urged the Confederate government to "take some…steps to protect…helpless families," the warning was primarily to Georgians already in the army. "Read this," the *Banner* told them, "and think in the hour of battle…of the fate that threatens all you hold dear!"[35]

Of course, thinking too much about threats to their loved ones might tempt Confederate soldiers to desert, as detailed in a brief story in the *Atlanta Southern Confederacy* in February 1863. An unnamed soldier's wife, "looking alone upon the dark side of the picture…magnified her troubles and sufferings" at home in a letter to her husband. The letter had a distressing effect on its recipient, who "became restless, discontented, unhappy" and "shutting his eyes to the consequences…*deserted!*" Recaptured, the soldier was executed. "His wife," the paper lamented, "is now a widow[,] tortured with the thought that her husband was brought to an untimely end by her own imprudence."[36] To avoid such a fate, Georgia's women were advised to "say nothing" in their letters that "may embitter [the soldiers'] thoughts, weaken their arms, depress their courage, or tempt them from the path of patriotic duty."[37] Of course, women did not always follow this policy, as

[35] *Athens Southern Banner,* 11 March 1863.
[36] *Atlanta Southern Confederacy,* 11 February 1863.
[37] Ibid.

evidenced by the depressing tone of so much Civil War correspondence. And men continued to slip away from the Confederate Army, although the desertions generally were not reported in Georgia newspapers.

That some Southern women were urging their men to desert suggests all was not well in Georgia in March 1863. Even though Federal soldiers might be far away, and Confederate armies might be winning victories, there were still great troubles at hand. Sabotage, Unionist sentiment, and outright rebellions disturbed the peace.

In some parts of the state, there was great fear of Yankee sabotage. A number of Georgia residents, especially those in large cities such as Atlanta, Augusta, Macon, and Savannah, were of Northern birth, and though many of them had become Southerners at heart, others remained Unionists. Fires and rumors of slave uprisings were often pinned on these transplants, fostering a sense of paranoia amongst Georgia's Confederates.[38]

Railroad bridges were considered special targets of saboteurs. In early March, the *Atlanta Intelligencer* related an incident in which a Confederate guard on a Chattahoochee River bridge near Atlanta apprehended a stranger trying to cross in the morning hours. The stranger identified himself as a local track hand, but the guard, suspicious of the man's "contradictory statements made, and ignorance on the questions propounded to him," tried to take him to Atlanta. Breaking free, the stranger ran away, hotly pursued by almost a half-dozen Confederates. "These…would soon have overtaken him," the paper reported, "had not one of the guards stumbled, by which act his piece was [accidentally] discharged," wounding two of the soldiers. The *Intelligencer*

---

[38] T. Conn Bryan, *Confederate Georgia* (Athens: University of Georgia Press, 1953) 137–39.

regretted the suspect's escape, concluding that "too much vigilance cannot be exercised by those in charge of our railroad bridges."[39]

Even amongst the native-born, white population there was never universal support of the Confederacy. Fond sympathies for the Union or resentment of the plantation aristocracy fed discontent among some Georgians. These anti-Confederates, often from lower economic classes, resented having to take part in what they saw as a "rich man's war, poor man's fight." Torn from homes and families by the draft, taxed beyond their means by the Confederate government, and relentlessly hunted if they deserted from the army, dissenters in Georgia went into hiding or became guerrilla fighters. Such internecine conflict consumed men and resources that might have gone to the Confederate frontlines. By 1863, Georgia, like many other Confederate states, was fighting a civil war within a civil war.[40]

Almost no mention of this internal dissension was made amongst major Georgia newspapers during spring 1863. However, recent studies have uncovered a seething cauldron of discontent. In the Chattahoochee River valley to the west and the Appalachian counties to the north, army deserters, Unionist guerrillas, and ordinary men and women violently resisted the Confederate government. Marauding bands along the Chattahoochee, led by Confederate deserters such as John Sanders and "Speckled" John Ward, looted plantations, terrorized pro-Confederate citizens, destroyed Confederate depots and fought Confederate army detachments. Meanwhile, the mountain counties of Fannin and Lumpkin suffered similar disorder, punctuated by violence on both sides. The situation had become so bad in the mountains that, in January 1863, Governor Brown had sent over 1,000 men under Colonel George W. Lee to round up the leaders of the

---

[39] *Atlanta Intelligencer,* 5 March 1863.
[40] Bryan, *Confederate Georgia,* 139–55.

resistance and restore order. Even in Atlanta, there were rumblings. Only a few weeks after the 66th Georgia advertised for recruits in the newspapers, a small number of hungry, angry Southern women caused a riot in the city, threatening storekeepers and stealing foodstuffs.[41]

Although this resistance challenges postwar myths about complete Southern solidarity behind the Confederacy, wartime dissent in Georgia should not be overemphasized. Anti-Confederate gangs in the Chattahoochee valley were still relatively small in mid-1863, and they were not able to seriously disrupt the industrial output of the region. Colonel Lee's expedition stamped out much of the anti-Confederate resistance in Fannin and Lumpkin, even though the ringleaders returned to make more trouble. And the women's riots in Atlanta were mostly meant to shame the national government into giving better assistance to soldiers' families; by and large, they were not intended as protests against the Confederacy itself. While dissent in Georgia would increase as Confederate armies lost battles and Union forces penetrated the state, confidence in victory and support for the Confederacy remained high during spring 1863.

The question of how many men were left to serve in units such as the 66th cannot be conclusively answered. Several thousand men were in the Georgia militia, which suggests a small reservoir of untapped manpower. Yet many of the militia were very young, very old, physically infirm, or incapacitated.[42] And evidence, albeit

---

[41] David Williams, *Rich Man's War: Class, Caste, and Confederate Defeat in the Lower Chattahoochee River Valley* (Athens: University of Georgia Press, 1998) 144–50; Jonathan Dean Sarris, *A Separate Civil War: Communities in Conflict in the Mountain South* (Charlottesville: University of Virginia Press, 2006) 65–66, 88–100; Williams, Williams, and Carlson, *Plain Folk in a Rich Man's War,* 71–90.

[42] William R. Scaife and William Harris Bragg, *Joe Brown's Pets: The Georgia Militia, 1862–1865* (Macon: Mercer University Press, 2004) passim.

from a later date, suggests that Confederate manpower was rapidly drying up. Conscription officials reporting in 1864 concluded that the Confederate states had sent about as many men as they could into the army.[43]

When the 66th Georgia was formed, the state press, both reflecting and molding popular opinion, expected that the Confederacy would yet win. There might be problems to resolve, especially in regards to taxes and food. Opinion might be divided about whether victory might come through battles, European intervention, or Northern exhaustion. Some of Georgia's citizens might be growing restless under the Confederate yoke. Even so, the picture was not completely bleak. Confederate armies were either winning or holding their own, Union forces were not ravaging Georgia, and most citizens seemed willing to pay any price for victory.

Early in March 1863, when the Yankees menaced Fort McAllister, Governor Brown had called for volunteers to bolster the fort's garrison. The result, according to the *Augusta Chronicle*, was heartwarming to Confederate patriots. "From every quarter…in almost every city and town…movements are on foot for the organization of companies. Old men, whose sons are in the armies of Virginia and the West, are ready to come at the first signal of alarm." Victory was assured, the paper promised, "while such a spirit animates our people."[44] In a similar spirit, and with ambition in his heart, a young man from Macon named James C. Nisbet, seasoned and anxious for a new command, came home to raise his state's last Confederate infantry regiment.

---

[43] Gary W. Gallagher, *The Confederate War* (Cambridge: Harvard University Press, 1999) 34–35.

[44] *Augusta Chronicle,* 4 March 1863.

Chapter 2

Nisbet's Officers:
The Colonel and the Veterans

James C. Nisbet

Alongside the advertisement for the formation of the 66th Georgia Infantry, a correspondent for the *Macon Telegraph* assessed the regiment's intended commander: "Captain Nisbet, though young, has seen as much active service as most veterans of three score. He has…fought twenty battles, in which he has displayed heroic bravery… His reputation for coolness and gallantry in danger and for general efficiency as a military officer is exceeded by no man…"[1] Though the article betrayed some home-town favoritism, it did not much exaggerate the captain's qualifications. James Cooper Nisbet was indeed young, brave, experienced and efficient. Twenty-four years old when he became a colonel, Nisbet stood 5 feet, 10 inches tall, had dark hair and blue eyes, and came from Scottish stock. His ancestors included Murdoch Nisbet, a sixteenth-century martyr of the Reformation, and John Nisbet, one of Oliver Cromwell's soldiers who was captured and executed during the English Civil War. John Nisbet's grandson had brought the family to America in 1730. The succeeding Nisbet generations had settled in Georgia, raised cotton, practiced law, and served in Congress.[2]

---

[1] *Milledgeville Confederate Union,* 24 March 1863.

[2] James C. Nisbet compiled service record (CSR), 21st Georgia Infantry, National Archives and Records Administration (NARA), Washington, DC (All CSR citations are for the 66th Georgia Infantry unless otherwise noted.); James

Nisbet was born on 26 September 1839, to Macon attorney James Alexander Nisbet and his wife Frances. Little is known about Nisbet's early life. After three years of college prep at a Rome, Georgia high school, Nisbet had apparently attended Oglethorpe University in Milledgeville.[3] Upon his graduation, Nisbet had moved to Dade County in 1859 and established Cloverdale Stock Farm, although in the 1860 census he was still listed as living with his parents. Stock-raising did not prove to be an immediately lucrative business for the young Georgian; while the census listed his father with a $35,000 estate, Nisbet was shown as having no real or personal property.[4]

After the attack on Fort Sumter, Nisbet had tried to join the "Raccoon Roughs," a company of mountain men raised by neighbor and future Confederate general John Brown Gordon. Gordon had encouraged Nisbet to raise his own company instead. Nisbet had quickly gathered eighty-five recruits and left for Virginia in July 1861, arriving in Richmond too late for the First Battle of Manassas. There, Nisbet's group had become Company H of the 21st Georgia Infantry, under Colonel John T. Mercer. That regiment had ended up in the Confederate Army of Northern Virginia, under Generals Robert E. Lee and Thomas J. "Stonewall" Jackson.[5] For the next year and a half, Nisbet had participated in campaigns in the Shenandoah Valley, Middle and Northern Virginia, and Maryland, and had often been in the thick of the fighting. Proud of his regiment's record, Nisbet later

C. Nisbet, *Four Years on the Firing Line* (Chattanooga TN: Imperial Press, 1911) 6–8. All ages given are for 1863, unless otherwise noted.

[3] Nisbet's name does not appear in the university's 1859 catalog of graduates.

[4] *Atlanta Weekly Constitution,* 17 July 1877; Nisbet, *Four Years,* 17–19; Eighth Census, 1860, Georgia, free inhabitants, Bibb County. Nisbet claimed that he was a slave owner by 1861 (Nisbet, *Four Years,* 69).

[5] Nisbet, *Four Years,* 34–43.

boasted that the 21st Georgia had seen more action than any other Confederate unit.[6]

Captain Nisbet's first year of service had been mostly unexceptional. It was not until the second summer of the war that Nisbet distinguished himself. At Gaines' Mill, Virginia (27 June 1862), during the Seven Days' Battles, the young captain had proved his mettle while temporarily in command of the full 21st Georgia. As a newspaper reported, the regiment had initially balked at Nisbet's repeated orders to charge a strong, entrenched Federal position. Trying once again, Nisbet,

> with the tact of an older General…orders up…his own company. He knew his men. *"Now,"* he shouts, *"I'll show you how to charge!"* And seizing the banner in his own hand, and waving his sword over his head, he shouts in a ringing voice—*"Forward, charge."*… Like an avalanche his men follow; and terror-stricken the Federals fly, leaving behind their standard and nine guns as the trophies…[7]

In the official reports of the Seven Days' campaign, Nisbet had been commended alongside five other officers of the 21st Georgia for "having shown conspicuous bravery."[8]

Nearly three months later, at Antietam, Maryland (17 September 1862), Nisbet had once again temporarily led the 21st. In one charge, Nisbet had been "struck in the stomach by a spent minie ball" and also wounded in his hand. Nisbet claimed that a surgeon examined the wounds and ordered him across the nearby Potomac River to recuperate. Far from praising his substitute's

---

[6] Ibid., 41, 136.

[7] *Macon Daily Telegraph*, 26 July 1862.

[8] US War Department, *The War of the Rebellion: A Compilation of the Official Records of the Union and Confederate Armies* (Washington, DC: US Government Printing Office, 1880–1901) vol. 11, pt. 2, p. 606 (Hereafter cited as *OR*; all citations are from series 1 unless otherwise noted.).

bravery at Antietam, Colonel Mercer had tried to convince Georgia newspapers that Nisbet had never been in the battle. Mercer had later acknowledged that Nisbet had been wounded, but insisted that his wounds were merely a "frivolous pretext" for Nisbet to abandon the battlefield.[9]

Perhaps jealous of Nisbet's notoriety, Colonel Mercer had continued to persecute the captain. Soon, Nisbet had faced other "charges of a serious character" filed by his commander. According to Mercer, Nisbet had left camp without authorization on 23 November 1862, while the army was near Madison Court House, Virginia. Taking along another officer and several privates of the 21st Georgia, Nisbet had allegedly gone on a "drunken debauch" lasting for several days, and culminating in a visit to a "habitation of lewd women" where Nisbet had acted "in the most indecent and scandalous manner." Furthermore, Mercer had charged Nisbet with helping one of his own men to desert by smuggling the man to a railroad station in an army ambulance.[10]

Nisbet had disputed these accusations, claiming that he left camp with Mercer's permission, to pick up boxes of extra clothing for his men. When Nisbet returned, Mercer had placed him under arrest. "Colonel Mercer said he did not remember giving me permission to leave camp," Nisbet wrote, "which may have been true, as he was under the influence of the 'rosy' at the time."[11]

Who was telling the truth? Certainly countless soldiers in the Civil War indulged in drinking and womanizing. Perhaps Nisbet too had succumbed to temptation. If so, he would have been understandably loath to make a full confession in his memoirs. On

---

[9] *Macon Daily Telegraph*, 11 October 1862; Nisbet CSR, 21st Georgia; Nisbet, *Four Years*, 153, 162.

[10] Nisbet CSR, 21st Georgia.

[11] Nisbet, *Four Years*, 55. Nisbet incorrectly dates the incident to November 1861.

the other hand, Mercer's attacks against Nisbet might have been a smokescreen to mask Mercer's own deficiencies. As Nisbet noted, Mercer himself had a weakness for liquor. In fact, it was Mercer's intoxication at Gaines' Mill that had forced Nisbet to assume command of the regiment.[12] A few weeks after Nisbet's supposed indecencies, Mercer had been tried for cowardice under fire and other failings and exonerated. By spring 1863, however, many of Mercer's captains believed that he was unfit to command, and they petitioned in vain to have him relieved.[13]

Nisbet took a long leave of absence in early 1863 and went back to Macon. He was probably tired of Mercer's vendetta and looking for a way to escape it.[14] No longer content with being a mere captain toiling away under a difficult colonel, Nisbet had his sights on a higher rank and a more favorable position. As far as Nisbet was concerned, the 21st Georgia had become a dead end for his ambitions. Colonel Mercer was sure to block any promotions for Nisbet. Moreover, Nisbet claimed that the other captains were his seniors. Though Nisbet had occasionally commanded the 21st Georgia, he did not believe that he was the favored successor to Mercer.[15] If the young Georgian wanted permanent command of a regiment, he would have to create one himself. Earlier that winter, Nisbet had learned that some officers were trying to organize new military units in Georgia. Nisbet announced his intention to do likewise.

---

[12] Nisbet, *Four Years*, 110.

[13] Ibid., 55; Ujanirtus Allen to Susan Allen, 6 April 1863, in Randall Allen & Keith S. Bohannon, eds., *Campaigning with "Old Stonewall": Confederate Captain Ujanirtus Allen's Letters to His Wife* (Baton Rouge: Louisiana State University Press, 1998) 222.

[14] Allen attributed Nisbet's leave of absence to "an unwillingness to serve under Col M[ercer]," ibid, 222.

[15] Nisbet, *Four Years*, 185–86.

In February, Nisbet wrote General Howell Cobb, commander of Confederate forces in Georgia and Florida, and asked permission to raise a regiment. Cobb reminded Nisbet that only the Confederate War Department could provide such authorization, but promised to "most cheerfully recommend" a commission for Nisbet. "I trust you will succeed," Cobb encouraged the captain, "both in getting the authority and raising the regiment."[16]

Though he was still very young, Nisbet had a few aces in his hand apart from Cobb's recommendation. He was an officer with combat experience gained under Lee and Jackson, two of the Confederacy's most prominent and successful military leaders. More importantly, Nisbet had political connections. His uncle, Eugenius A. Nisbet, was a well-known state judge and prominent Confederate congressman. On 3 March 1863, Nisbet received the telegram he had been waiting for, granting him the authority to recruit a regiment for Cobb's District of Middle Florida.

Nisbet went to work. "I...established my headquarters in Macon...published my authority in all the daily papers...[and] visited many counties in Georgia." In his bustle of activity, Nisbet ended up overstaying his leave. Richmond pointed out the lapse in April, Nisbet was told to either return to duty at once or else resign his commission.[17] Nisbet did not immediately respond; his delay probably stemmed from the distractions and challenges of his new command. Spring 1863 was a difficult time for Nisbet. Initially restricted to recruiting in lower Georgia, he found plenty of would-be officers but few privates. Many of those who did join

---

[16] Howell Cobb to James Cooper Nisbet, 17 February 1863, Nisbet CSR, 21st Georgia.

[17] Richmond to Howell Cobb, 3 March 1863, Letters and Telegrams Sent by the Confederate Adjutant General and Inspector General, NARA; Nisbet, *Four Years,* 186; Richmond to Cobb, 24 April 1863, Letters and Telegrams Sent by the Confederate Adjutant General and Inspector General, NARA.

up were dragged off by Confederate conscription officers to other postings.[18] Without men in the ranks, the 66th Georgia would die stillborn. As his uncle noted, Nisbet was "very anxious" to succeed but felt that unless he could recruit from the entire state, without hindrance from the draft, he "can not do it." While Eugenius pulled strings to expand his nephew's sphere of authority, Richmond expressed displeasure with Nisbet's continued absence and his lack of communication. "The vacancy in [Company H] must be filled," Confederate Adjutant General Samuel Cooper reminded him, "and unless [Nisbet] can make some report of the formation of his Regiment, he must return to his company."[19]

Later that summer, Nisbet finally resigned from the 21st Georgia, claiming that he had "three companies in camp & the others will soon rendezvous [at Macon]." Nisbet's commander was not so eager to let him go. Three months before, Colonel Mercer had brought charges against Nisbet for the alleged dalliances with liquor and women. "Several attempts have been made to secure his return to trial," Mercer wrote on Nisbet's resignation, which he endorsed, "Respectfully forwarded, disapproved." To Mercer's frustration, no doubt, Nisbet was never tried. The resignation was accepted by brigade commander General George P. Doles on 5 August, and by Major Walter H. Taylor, the adjutant of the Army of Northern Virginia, the following day.[20] Freed from the 21st Georgia, Captain Nisbet could become Colonel Nisbet.

---

[18] Nisbet, *Four Years*, 186–87.

[19] Eugenius A. Nisbet to Governor Jomison, 24 February 1863, Nisbet CSR; Samuel Cooper to Cobb, 17 June 1863, Letters and Telegrams Sent by the Confederate Adjutant General and Inspector General, NARA.

[20] James C. Nisbet to Samuel Cooper, 24 July 1863, Nisbet CSR; Mercer endorsement, 4 August 1863, Doles and Taylor endorsements, 5 and 6 August, 1863 Nisbet CSR.

Nisbet knew exactly what he wanted for his fledgling command: a core of experienced soldiers and a cadre of handpicked, competent officers. Veterans could quickly mold Nisbet's raw recruits into effective fighting men, while capable majors, captains, and lieutenants could keep the regiment running smoothly. To this end, the young commander tried to take a couple of companies (including his own) away from the 21st Georgia, as a nucleus for the new regiment. Moreover, Nisbet sought to appoint his own junior officers. "I had become convinced," Nisbet later explained, "...that the former method of electing officers could not be relied on at this stage of the struggle. To have an efficient regiment, it was necessary that the commissioned officers should be veterans, and otherwise qualified."[21]

Nisbet's efforts did not succeed to the degree that he had wished. Colonel Mercer, having lost the chance to prosecute Nisbet, was not about to part with his own forces. If Nisbet took away the two companies, Mercer complained to the Confederate War Department, the 21st Georgia would be reduced to a battalion, leaving Mercer with a command too small for his rank. Richmond quickly issued a veto. Nisbet would not be allowed to deplete the ranks of the 21st Georgia in order to fill the 66th. "Col. Mercer...forestalled us," Nisbet wrote in his memoirs, "so all we could do was to go to Georgia, and get busy recruiting" from scratch.[22]

Nisbet later remembered winning the right to appoint officers. After being stymied by Confederate Secretary of War James Seddon, who "would not consent that I should have the appointments," Nisbet took his case directly to Jefferson Davis. Face-to-face with the Confederate president, Nisbet begged for the freedom to "select soldiers, or ex-soldiers, for commissioned officers...

---

[21] Nisbet, *Four Years*, 187.
[22] Ibid., 188–89.

and if any of them were in the army, to have them detached for recruiting service."

According to Nisbet, Davis was at first reluctant to grant this authority. Nisbet, Davis opined, was too young to be a colonel. Governor Brown was hostile to further Confederate recruitment in Georgia, and other officers had recently failed to raise new units. Turning to Nisbet's uncle, Eugenius, who had gained Nisbet the interview, Davis asked, "Do you think the young man can raise a regiment in Georgia, at this time?" Eugenius did not hesitate to say yes. His nephew had "a good war record, energy, and family influence; if he can get the order he wants, I believe he will soon raise the regiment." That decided the matter. Davis immediately ordered Secretary Seddon to grant Nisbet's request, and when the 66th Georgia went off to war, Nisbet claimed, all of the regiment's officers and at least half of its enlisted men were veterans.[23] Notwithstanding whatever might have been said in the interview, Nisbet in fact did not get the authority he sought. Even if Davis's zealous protection of presidential prerogative was not an issue, the power to commission officers rested with the Confederate Congress. While Nisbet could select the regiment's executive officer and a few administrative officers, he was not given unlimited powers of appointment. On the contrary, the majority of Nisbet's officers acquired rank through the "vicious system of election" that Nisbet deplored.[24] So much for the dramatic gloss of Nisbet's postwar recollections.

More importantly, Nisbet did not succeed in placing experienced men at the head of each company. Of forty-one captains and lieutenants in the 66th Georgia, only sixteen were veterans. Fortunately for Nisbet, another twenty-five men with some experience joined the regiment as non-commissioned officers

---

[23] Ibid, 188, 289.
[24] Ibid., 187.

and privates. Though these forty-one veterans fell far short of comprising half of the regiment, as Nisbet claimed, they almost certainly made it easier for Nisbet to organize and train the 66th Georgia.

Algernon S. Hamilton

In Nisbet's opinion, only one veteran was capable enough to become his executive officer. Algernon Sidney Hamilton, five years Nisbet's senior, was an old friend from before the war. A doctor's son, Hamilton had left his family in Rome to attend the Georgia Military Institute in Marietta, before joining a filibuster (an extralegal paramilitary expedition) to Cuba that that ended up going no further south than Florida.[25]

The 1856 Kansas-Nebraska Act, which potentially opened up that vast territory to the South's "peculiar institution" of slavery, turned Hamilton's restless eyes westward. Taking along his brothers, Charles and Peter, as well as several slaves, Hamilton had tried to settle down there, only to sour on his new home when the internal war that defined "Bloody Kansas" proved too deadly. Expecting a fair fight, Hamilton had been dismayed "when the [antislavery forces] commenced to do secret murder—slaying sleeping households in their beds"—tactics employed by proslavery forces as well. Hamilton had quickly decamped to Texas and, like Nisbet, started a livestock business, before finally returning to Georgia.[26]

By 1860, Hamilton had become a middle-class businessman in Rome, with $8,500 in personal and real estate. In a bit of *noblesse oblige*, he had even rented out some of his property to the family of an unemployed mechanic and a widower with a child. When

---

[25] *Brief Biographies of the Members of the Constitutional Convention, July 11, 1877* (Atlanta: Constitution Publishing Co., 1877) 104.

[26] Nisbet, *Four Years*, 17–18.

the war came, Hamilton had joined the Confederate Army and raised a company, known as the Floyd Sharpshooters. To equip his men, Captain Hamilton had taken several dozen muskets from a state arsenal in Rome. An irate Governor Brown had demanded that the Confederate government order Hamilton to return the weapons to Georgia; President Davis had refused to do so.[27]

In Virginia, the Floyd Sharpshooters had become Company B of the 21st Georgia, reuniting Hamilton and Nisbet under Colonel Mercer. Hamilton had impressed fellow captain Ujanirtus Allen, who pronounced him "one of the nicest men you ever saw full [of] dry wit, and somewhat of an oddity in his way." Hamilton's relationship with the colonel had been less amiable. Within a year, Hamilton had called Mercer "a very dissolute character" and sought a transfer: "I don't want to. . . remain under him."[28] Six months of hard campaigning had left Hamilton little time to pursue his relief. The struggle against Mercer had resumed when the army went into winter camp. At Mercer's trial in December 1862, Hamilton had taken the stand for the prosecution and minced no words. "I there stated under oath," Hamilton said, "that...[Mercer] had shirked fights, and was a coward." After Mercer had been acquitted, Hamilton had decided that his days with the 21st Georgia were numbered. Having made an enemy of his commanding officer, he, like Nisbet, had little hope for promotion within the regiment. The day after Christmas, Hamilton had attempted to resign.[29]

---

[27] Ibid.; Eighth Census, 1860, Georgia, Free inhabitants, Floyd County; *OR*, ser. 4, vol. 1, p. 401.

[28] Ujanirtus Allen to Susan Allen, 25 December 1862, in *Campaigning with "Old Stonewall"*, 201; Algernon S. Hamilton to A. R. Wright, 15 June 1862, Letters Received by the Confederate Secretary of War, NARA.

[29] A. R. Wright to Thomas W. Hooper, 26 December 1862, Algernon S. Hamilton CSR, 21st Georgia Infantry. Allen, for one, expected Hamilton to be

Initially, his request had been denied. General Lee had found Hamilton's "grounds of ill-feeling" between himself and Colonel Mercer insufficient cause for relief. "I cannot for such reasons recommend acceptance," Lee had written. Hamilton, however, had been determined to be free of "embarrassing circumstances I deem intolerable." He had renewed his request for relief in early 1863, enlisting the support of the regiment's lieutenant colonel, "who recommends me as a true and faithful soldier, in the defense of my country."[30] Hamilton's pleas for "simple justice in my troubles" had earned him the sympathy of fellow Georgian and Confederate congressman Augustus Wright. "Permit me…to remark," Wright had observed, "that no man of his age outranks Cap't Hamilton as a gentleman of honor & a true soldier." Given Mercer's propensity for intoxication and his "overbearing and offensive" manner, if Hamilton stayed in the 21st Georgia, the situation would be "humiliating, not only to himself but to his family." Wright had further ventured a criticism of General Lee, "so accurate normally in his official action," for turning down Hamilton's request.[31]

After some time, Secretary of War Seddon ended Hamilton's service in Virginia and, in Special Order 127, dated 28 May 1863, assigned the captain to General P. G. T. Beauregard's Department of South Carolina, Florida, and Georgia. There, Hamilton helped Nisbet assemble the companies of the 66th Georgia. "Hamilton

---

promoted if Mercer was ever cashiered (*Campaigning with "Old Stonewall,"* 137).

[30] Lee endorsement, 30 December 1862, Wright to Hooper, Hamilton CSR, 21st Georgia Infantry.

[31] A. R. Wright to James A. Seddon, 22 January 1863, Hamilton CSR, 21st Georgia Infantry.

was happy" with his new assignment, Nisbet remembered. "No more weary marches on foot…and home!"[32]

Robert N. Hull

Nisbet lost his first choice for major of the 66th Georgia when the unnamed candidate opted instead for a "bomb-proof position" in Richmond. Instead, the rank of third in command initially fell to John Andrews, about whom little is known. When attrition thinned out the regiment's officer corps, Robert Newton Hull, a veteran of the 26th Georgia Infantry, became the new major. Twenty years old, Hull had been a printer by profession, living with a wealthy Dougherty County planter in 1860. As a lieutenant in the 26th, Hull had often been absent on furlough and recruiting duty, and apparently had seen little fighting.[33] More than likely, Hull's veteran status and skill as a drill master and recruiter helped him form Company A of the 66th Georgia, of which he was elected captain. If Nisbet had any reservations about Hull's lack of combat experience, he kept them to himself.

Officers from the Doles-Cook Brigade

During Nisbet's leave in winter 1862, his parent brigade in the Army of Northern Virginia was reorganized. The 12th and 21st Georgia were joined by the 4th and 44th to form a brigade under General George P. Doles. Almost one-quarter of Nisbet's veterans originally served in this all-Georgia brigade, later known as the

---

[32] Unfiled items, Hamilton CSR, 21st Georgia Infantry; Nisbet, *Four Years,* 188, 191.

[33] Nisbet, *Four Years*, 189–90, Eighth Census, 1860, Georgia, free inhabitants, Dougherty County; Robert N. Hull CSR, 26th Georgia Infantry.

"Doles-Cook Brigade."[34] Apart from Hamilton, only a few gained rank in the 66th Georgia.

Captain Alexander Reid and Lieutenant Josiah Flournoy Adams of Company F both came from the 12th Georgia Infantry. Known as the "Bloody Twelfth," this regiment had made a determined and costly stand at the Battle of McDowell, Virginia (8 May 1862). Nisbet would have been familiar with the unit, though he might not have known either Reid, a mere private, or Adams, a sergeant who had been absent sick during every major campaign.[35]

The seven veterans from the 4th and 44th Georgia were a similarly undistinguished lot. Few of them had spent much time in service. James Turner had left the 4th in August 1861, a soldier for only four months; Stephen Mann of the 44th had received a discharge the following May for disability; and James Lancaster and Thomas Leverett of the same unit had left later in 1862. Serious illness had ended the services of others. Jason Dupree had become "a confirmed consumptive" in the opinion of the surgeon who discharged him in August 1862, while James Merritt had spent a lot of time in the hospital for chronic rheumatism and diarrhea. William Morgan Weaver had been a reasonably healthy sergeant in the 44th, but within a few months of joining, he had furnished a substitute and quit. Ill, unmotivated or homesick earlier in the war, these seven men chose to fight again under

---

[34] Henry W. Thomas, *History of The Doles-Cook Brigade, Army of Northern Virginia, C.S.A.* (Atlanta: Franklin Printing & Publishing Co., 1903). Nisbet, Hamilton, and others who later joined the 66th Georgia are mentioned only in passing.

[35] Josiah F. Adams CSR, and Alexander H. Reid CSR, 12th Georgia Infantry; Keith S. Bohannon, "'Placed On the Pages of History in Letters of Blood': Reporting On and Remembering the 12th Georgia Infantry in the 1862 Valley Campaign," in *The Shenandoah Valley Campaign of 1862*, ed. Gary W. Gallagher (Chapel Hill: UNC Press, 2003) 115–43.

Nisbet. Weaver, Leverett, and Mann, at least, gained promotions in the 66th, to lieutenant, sergeant, and corporal respectively. The other four remained enlisted men.[36]

Officers from the 3rd Georgia Infantry

The Doles-Cook Brigade was not the only source of veterans for the 66th Georgia. The 3rd Georgia Infantry of the Army of Northern Virginia contributed seven soldiers to the 66th Georgia, more than any other single early-war unit. This is not so surprising given that Nisbet's cousin, Reuben Nisbet, was lieutenant colonel of the 3rd for most of the war.

Many of the veterans from the 3rd knew how to fight and how to lead. Several also bore physical reminders of bloody battles. Sergeant Henry Parks, like Nisbet, had been wounded at Antietam. So had Isaac Reese, an ensign with a second wound from Chancellorsville, Virginia (1–3 May 1863). Still others were formerly officers, such as George Hall, a captain who later was elected to the same rank in Company G of the 66th. Despite their lower ranks in the 3rd, Parks and Reese also became company officers under Nisbet.[37]

Officers from the 2nd Georgia Infantry Battalion

Though the 3rd Georgia gave the most men, the 2nd Georgia Infantry Battalion gave Nisbet most of his veteran company officers. Like the 3rd Georgia, this unit had served under Lee in Virginia, but in contrast to the veterans of the 3rd, Charles Holmes, Briggs Napier, William LeConte, William Ross, and

---

[36] CSRs for Jason Dupree, James Lancaster , Thomas Leverett, and Stephen Mann, 44th Georgia Infantry; CSRs for James Merritt, James A. Turner, and William M. Weaver, 4th Georgia Infantry.

[37] Nisbet, *Four Years*, 157; CSRs for George A. Hall, Henry F. Parks, and Isaac W. Reese, 3rd Georgia Infantry.

Charles Williamson, all privates in the 2nd Georgia Battalion, had earned no distinctions in combat. Why then did Williamson become a captain, and the others lieutenants, in the 66th Georgia?

In part, their appointments reflected high social status. The ranks of the 2nd Georgia Battalion were filled with the sons of many prominent families from Columbus and Macon. Quite a few were professionals—doctors, lawyers, and businessmen—or had served in prewar militia units. Such men were considered the future leaders of Georgia, eminently qualified for positions of authority.

Some veterans of the 2nd Georgia Battalion, such as William LeConte, had met Nisbet in the Army of Northern Virginia. LeConte was approached by Nisbet in spring 1863, but initially declined to join Nisbet's new regiment. "We [in Lee's army] were then about to start on this trip of invasion," Leconte later explained, "and I was not willing to come home; I felt as though it would look *badly*." After the "trip of invasion," culminating in Confederate defeat at Gettysburg, Pennsylvania (1–3 July 1863), and subsequent retreat, LeConte felt differently. Offered a position as adjutant of the 66th Georgia—along with a thirty-day furlough—LeConte burned his old, lice-infested clothes, had a new uniform tailored, and joined Nisbet in Macon.[38]

Briggs H. Napier

A close examination of Briggs Napier's service record suggests that persistence and political connections helped some men gain commissions in Nisbet's new regiment. Born into a wealthy family, Napier had been sent to Europe at the outbreak of the war, according to his daughter, "to lead [him] out of the temptation of volunteering." Disregarding his father's instructions to stay

---

[38] William L. Leconte, "Events of My Life," unpublished memoirs, private collection, 20.

abroad, Napier had soon returned home and joined the 2nd Georgia Battalion in May 1861. For several months, the battalion was at Norfolk, Virginia, guarding the nearby Confederate naval base at Gosport. Napier's health had quickly taken a turn for the worse; he had been absent sick from late summer all the way through to winter. In an attempt to recuperate, Napier had gone home to Macon, but had not gotten better. Citing "repeated attacks of intermittent fever, together with a delicacy of constitution & susceptibility of the lungs to disease," the battalion commander had approved Napier's discharge for disability in January 1862.[39]

Napier had rejected being declared an invalid and forced out of service. Within a few weeks of his discharge, he had joined his brother's Georgia artillery battery as a lieutenant. Once again, Napier had been posted on the coast, at Savannah. This time, the sea air had seemed to restore his broken health. The prospect of serving out the war in mundane garrison duties, however, had not appealed to Napier. In mid-April, Napier had written to President Davis requesting a promotion. Davis did not respond.[40]

Discouraged but not dismayed, Napier had sought a transfer to the Western Theater in summer 1862. Union forces in that theater, under Generals Ulysses S. Grant and Don Carlos Buell, had overrun most of Tennessee and had been steadily pushing down the Mississippi River valley. The Confederate Army of Mississippi, having been defeated by Grant and Buell at Shiloh (6–7 April 1862), had retreated from the crucial railroad junction

---

[39] Gladys Napier Corbin, "Reminiscences of Briggs Hopson Napier," in *Reminiscences of Confederate Soldiers and Stories of the War* (United Daughters of the Confederacy, 1940) vol. XII, 220; Briggs H. Napier CSR, 2nd Georgia Infantry Battalion.

[40] Napier to Jefferson Davis, 17 April 1862, Napier CSR, 2nd Georgia Battalion.

at Corinth, Mississippi, south to Tupelo, where it had licked its wounds and waited for the next campaign.

Napier had seen the Western Theater as a place to start afresh, smell gunpowder, and gain rank. Hastening to Tupelo, Napier had arrived in June with a letter of introduction from Eugenius Nisbet. The Confederate congressman had urged General John C. Breckenridge, a commander in the Army of Mississippi, to find some duty for Napier. A month later, still without a post, Napier had written Breckenridge himself. He had wanted a position as volunteer aide-de-camp, but hinted that he was also qualified to be Breckenridge's chief of artillery.[41] Again, his petition had fallen on deaf ears.

The rest of 1862 had been as devoid of military glory for Napier as the year before. From Virginia to Maryland, from Mississippi to Tennessee and Kentucky, the Confederacy's armies had marched and fought, often snatching victory from the jaws of defeat. For Napier, though, no post of action had been found. To make some money, as well as to be more visible, Napier had turned to government work in the Confederate Treasury Department in Richmond. Clerking by day and reading military manuals by night, Napier had also cultivated powerful friends. Through Eugenius Nisbet, he had met Confederate Congressmen Benjamin Hill and Augustus Kennan of Georgia and Lucius Q. C. Lamar of Mississippi. Armed with references from these four, Napier had written to Davis again in October 1862, begging to be appointed a drillmaster: "For the last 14 months I have applied myself to the study of *Hardee*['s *Tactics*], & together with the instruction of my brother, who is a graduate of West Point, I

---

[41] Eugenius A. Nisbet to John C. Breckenridge, 9 June 1862, Napier CSR, 2nd Georgia Battalion; Napier to Breckenridge, 3 July 1862, Napier CSR, 2nd Georgia Battalion.

think I am competent to fill the post I now ask of you… If you cannot give me the position please let me know the reason why."[42]

The Confederate president could not help. "Return [to] Mr. Napier," Davis endorsed the pleading missive, "and say that drill masters are appointed upon the nomination of the commander of [the] camp of instruction."[43] Stuck in a menial and mind-numbing job, Napier had tried to make his situation more beneficial. When a higher-ranking, permanent clerk position had opened up at the Treasury Department in December, Napier had interviewed for it.[44] For a fifth time, Napier's hopes had been crushed, though this time he was fortunate to have been turned down. A few months later, James Nisbet posted his advertise-ments, and Napier, unhampered by other responsibilities and probably sponsored by Nisbet's uncle, sought and found a home in the officer corps of the 66th Georgia.

Officers from Ramsey's First Georgia Infantry

The 1st Regiment, Georgia Volunteer Infantry, known as Ramsey's 1st Georgia, also provided some of Nisbet's veteran company officers. Ramsey's 1st was actually older than the war itself, having been raised from militia companies in March 1861. Sent to western Virginia, the men of the regiment had hoped to have a role in a war-ending Southern victory. Instead, they had suffered defeats and stalemates in the summer and fall, had slogged through snow-covered mountains in the winter, and had heard tales of venomous squabblings between their brigade commander and "Stonewall"

---

[42] Napier to Jefferson Davis, 23 October 1862, Napier CSR, 2nd Georgia Battalion.
[43] Davis, endorsement, 4 November 1862, Napier CSR, 2nd Georgia Battalion.
[44] Napier to C. S. Memminger, 4 December 1862, Napier CSR, 2nd Georgia Battalion.

Jackson. The following spring, Ramsey's 1st had transferred to the western theater, but never got there. Colonel Ramsey had become sick and the one-year terms of service for his men had begun to expire, so the regiment had gone back to Georgia and disbanded in March 1862. Many of the regiment's men had quickly rejoined the Confederate Army in other units.[45]

Lieutenant Osborne Stone was the only veteran with rank in Ramsey's 1st to become an officer in the 66th. Stone, a twenty-six-year-old from Augusta, had become a corporal in September 1861, during the Cheat Mountain Campaign, and a sergeant three months later. After his regiment disbanded, Stone had joined the 12th Georgia Artillery Battalion, a home for many of Ramsey's former men, as a private on 10 April 1862.[46] Throughout the fall and winter, Stone had served on detached duty with the Confederate Commissary Department at Chattanooga, Tennessee. As with other Confederate veterans who joined Nisbet's regiment, Stone's main qualifications seem to have been prior service, familiarity with military procedures, and administrative skills.

None of Ramsey's other veterans had displayed any leadership qualities of note. Brothers John and Lorenzo Belisle had earned a bit of extra money as wagon drivers in western Virginia. Ellis Harrison Hull had switched from Ramsey's 1st to the 20th Georgia Infantry in late summer 1861, then fell sick; he had relapsed again after the 20th's baptism of fire in the Seven Days' Battles. Jesse Thornton had spent the year after his discharge doing very little to prepare for the command of Nisbet's Company

---

[45] George Winston Martin, *"I Will Give Them One More Shot": Ramsey's 1st Georgia Volunteers* (Macon, GA.: Mercer University Press, 2010) passim.

[46] Osborne M. Stone CSR, 1st Georgia Infantry (Ramsey's). Curiously, Stone's record has him joining the 63rd Georgia the same day. As the 63rd was not officially formed until later in the year, this is probably an error in transcription.

I, where his limited knowledge of duties would prove a liability.[47] Despite their somewhat undistinguished backgrounds, all of these men save John Belisle gained officer's commissions.

Officers from Various Georgia Units

The other veterans who served in the 66th Georgia came from the 2nd, 7th, 8th, 9th, 10th, 29th, 36th (Broyle's), 42nd and 53rd infantry regiments; the 1st Georgia State Troops; the 3rd Georgia Battalion; and Captain Tiller's Artillery Company. Six of these units had served under Lee in Virginia, but as with the other veterans mentioned above, it hardly seems possible that Nisbet personally knew the men who came from them. Some veterans of these Georgia units had seen combat, such as Moses L. Brown of the 7th, wounded at First Bull Run. Others, like Ascon Moody of the 29th, had been officers earlier in the war. Even so, most were no more noteworthy than countless others in the Confederate Army. Almost half of them had been sick for most of the early war. They boasted no commendations for service. On the plus side, many had at least one year of experience, which meant that they probably knew how to drill men, organize units, and handle army bureaucracy.

William T. Williams, Jr.

Apart from the veterans, one other soldier in the 66th Georgia had a background in military order and discipline. William Thorne Williams, Jr., the grandson of a Savannah engineer, had attended the Georgia Military Institute (GMI) early in the war. During his first year at the Institute, Williams had been made orderly sergeant in the corps of cadets. When Federal forces approached Chattanooga in fall 1863, Williams abruptly left the GMI and

---

[47] CSRs for John Belisle, Lorenzo D. Belisle, Ellis H. Hull, and Jesse Thornton, 1st Georgia Infantry (Ramsey's).

joined Company K of Nisbet's regiment as a private. He seems to have hoped to receive an appointment as a junior lieutenant. Recognizing his skills, Nisbet appointed Williams drillmaster, but did not recommend him for a promotion.[48]

Details from Williams's service record suggest that he did not adjust well to life in the field. Williams was listed as absent for much of 1863, and was eventually transferred from Company K to Company I, perhaps to assist Captain Thornton. In spite of his youth—Williams was only seventeen when he joined the 66th Georgia—he felt entitled to an officer's commission or a position as cadet in the regular Confederate Army. Unfortunately for Williams, he received neither. Judged unfit for field duty in March 1864, Williams left the 66th Georgia to serve as an artillery clerk in his home town.[49]

Summary

If James Cooper Nisbet had wanted a proven, battle-tested band of men to lead his new regiment, he did not get it. Most of his veterans were not officers, and most of his officers were not veterans. Few of them had been in combat, and even fewer had any command experience. By and large, Nisbet's veteran soldiers had quietly done their time earlier in the war, then left. Whether they were anxious to avoid being drafted, pleased to return to duty provided they stayed close to home, or eager to "see the elephant" in combat and maybe gain promotions, they chose a soldier's life again in 1863.

It bears repeating that Nisbet's soldiers, and not Nisbet, chose most of the officers of the 66th Georgia. Had Nisbet's powers been as broad as he later claimed, he might have picked a different

---

[48] William T. Williams, Jr., CSR; Eighth Census, 1860, Georgia, Free inhabitants, Chatham County.
[49] Williams CSR.

group of men. Of course, it may be that Nisbet's captains, lieutenants, sergeants, and corporals were simply the best available choices. Perhaps Nisbet's men felt that the right to vote for officers was more important than the specific qualifications of those officers.[50] Perhaps, too, they believed that ordinary, untrained citizens could be capable military leaders. What then of Nisbet's enlisted men, the bulk of whom were similarly untrained? Let us look at the social demographics of the regiment.

---

[50] According to Confederate veteran Isaac W. Avery, "there was no difficulty in Georgia about getting plenty of troops when they were allowed the privilege of organizing and electing their own…officers…This right of organization they considered…clearly guaranteed [to] them, and they set great store by it," Avery, *The History of the State of Georgia from 1850 to 1881* (New York: Brown & Derby Publishers, 1881) 231–32.

Chapter 3

The Rank and File:
Demographics of a Late-War Regiment

Charles Dupree had seemed likely to miss the Civil War. Sixteen years old in 1861, the Henry County, Georgia, youth was two years too young to fight in the Confederate army. No matter; by political string-pulling, bribery, or simply lying about his age, Dupree had managed to join Company D of the 6th Georgia Infantry as a private on 27 May 1861.[1] Known as the Butts County Volunteers, Company D drew largely from that one county, meaning that Dupree had been a bit of an outsider. In late summer 1861, the 6th Georgia had left for Virginia. Dupree had not accompanied the regiment; on a surgeon's recommendation, he had been discharged for "physical disability" in September 1861.[2]

Eighteen months had passed, during which his state mustered many more infantry regiments into Confederate service, while Dupree presumably remained home. Then came word that a new Georgia regiment would be created. Whatever had kept Dupree out of the war until that time, it was not enough to keep him from joining up once again. On 7 August 1863, Dupree became a first sergeant in the 66th Georgia Infantry.[3]

---

[1] Charles W. Dupree compiled service (CSR), 6th Georgia Infantry, National Archives and Records Administration (NARA), Washington, DC (All CSR citations are for the 66th Georgia Infantry unless otherwise noted.); Eighth Census, 1860, Georgia, free inhabitants, Henry County.

[2] Dupree CSR, 6th Georgia Infantry.

[3] Dupree CSR.

While Dupree's company formed in Macon that summer, the youthful sergeant might have studied his men. He would have noticed at least two differences between the Butts County Volunteers and Company D of the 66th Georgia. First, the soldiers of the 66th came from many different counties. Second, these new recruits were not youthful patriots like the men of the 6th Georgia. While Dupree and fellow sergeants James Dailey and Thomas Mitchell were still teenagers, more than two dozen of their men were thirty or older. Thus were the usual patterns of war reversed; in Company D of the 66th Georgia, the *young* would lead the *old* into battle.

Georgia sent men from the mountainous Upcountry, the Upper Piedmont, the Wiregrass plains, the fertile Plantation Belt, and the Low Country coast to serve alongside Sergeant Dupree.[4] Of 517 men in Nisbet's regiment found in the census records, 23 came from the Wiregrass, 59 came from the Upcountry, and 132 came from the Upper Piedmont. A mere six men came from the Lowcountry (See appendices A and B.). The majority of the men—288—came from the Plantation Belt.

Within these regions, Georgia's counties contributed varying amounts of manpower to the 66th. Among all counties represented, Newton was easily first, with at least forty-six men. Greene County ranked second, providing thirty-three men, while Putnam County was home for at least thirty others. Nineteen men each came from Walton and Madison County, and sixteen from

---

[4] This division of the state is borrowed from Mark Alan Weitz, "A Higher Duty: Desertion among Georgia Troops during the Civil War" (PhD Diss., Arizona State University, 1998).

Bibb County.[5] Altogether, these six counties supplied 163 men, almost one-third of the group.

Another seven Georgia counties sent at least ten men each into the ranks of the 66th Georgia. These were Dekalb County, with sixteen men; Morgan, with fifteen; Clarke and Habersham, with thirteen each; and Gwinnett and Hall, with twelve each. The regiment's remaining manpower was drawn rather unevenly from the rest of the state. Twenty-six counties supplied but one man each. Another twenty-one counties contributed two men each, and a final twenty-three other counties gave three to four men each.

In most early-war regiments, companies had been recruited from one or two counties each. Not so in the 66th Georgia; only a few companies were associated with specific counties. Company C, under Captain Henry F. Parks, drew forty-four men from Newton County, including one lieutenant and six non-commissioned officers. Captain Alexander H. Reid's Company F likewise recruited heavily from Putnam County; Reid, three lieutenants, three non-commissioned officers, and twenty-three of the company's enlisted men were residents. By contrast, most of the other companies included men from all over Georgia. Company H drew men from thirty-three different counties, while Company B represented twenty-nine counties and Companies A, D, and E all contained men from at least two dozen counties.

Typically Civil War soldiers are envisioned as no more than twenty-five years old, though in fact men of all ages served in the war. As often as not, boys too young to shave fought alongside grizzled old hands who could have been (and sometimes were)

---

[5] Anita B. Sams, *Wayfarers in Walton: A History of Walton County, Georgia, 1818–1967* (Monroe, GA: Walton Press, Inc., 1967) 125, claims that 26 men from Walton served in the regiment.

their fathers.[6] The ages for those in the 66th Georgia reflect this wide range. Irish-born Sergeant James Dailey, the youngest man in the group, was only fifteen years old when he joined the regiment. Company K's Lieutenant Benjamin Hammock was, at sixty-two, the oldest; he resigned during the Atlanta Campaign, realizing that he was too old to be an active soldier.[7] Between youngster Daily and oldster Hammock, nearly every age from sixteen to fifty-three was represented.

Thirty was the average age for Nisbet's men, while thirty-three was the median age. Yet the regiment had large numbers of men both far younger and somewhat older. Almost a quarter of the men found in the census were under twenty years of age, with eighteen and seventeen the two most common of all ages listed. Those between twenty and thirty years of age made up another quarter of the group. Far fewer men were in their early- to mid-thirties. In the late thirties and early forties, though, the numbers rose yet again. Forty-one and forty-two were the third and fourth most common ages listed. Altogether, 225 men (43 percent of the group) were between the ages of 35 and 45.[8]

Ninety-two men in the group were too young to serve legally in the Confederate army when the war began in 1861.[9] The other 400 new recruits were old enough to have enlisted at any time

---

[6] At least 25 brothers served together in Nisbet's regiment. Twelve fathers also served with their sons in the Sixty–Sixth Georgia, and a few fathers became non–commissioned officers in their sons' companies. Lillian Henderson, ed., *Roster of the Confederate Soldiers of Georgia,* vol. VI, 693–771.

[7] Eighth Census, 1860, Georgia, Free inhabitants, Chatham County; Ibid., Randolph County; James Dailey CSR; Benjamin F. Hammock CSR.

[8]In one survey, twenty–six was the average age of the Confederate soldiers that had enlisted in 1862 (Kenneth W. Noe, *Reluctant Rebels: The Confederates who Joined the Army After 1861* [Chapel Hill: University of North Carolina Press, 2010] 14–15).

[9]This counts only those not already in service and those without prior service.

before Colonel Nisbet began raising his regiment.[10] Kenneth Noe's *Reluctant Rebels* offers several explanations for their late enrollment. Some later-enlisting Confederates may have been sick or otherwise indisposed at the beginning of the war. Some might have signed up later in order to serve with friends or family members; the almost-uniform county demographics of the 66th Georgia's Companies C and F point to this. Some might have struggled with religious scruples against fighting and killing, while still others might have been determined to stay out of the war until compelled to fight. Finally, more than a few were probably reluctant to leave their families.[11]

Many men in the 66th Georgia could have claimed that family concerns kept them at home through 1861 and 1862. At least 242 of the men were married, and many of these husbands were fathers as well; another nine appear to have been widowers.[12] On average, fathers in the group had at least four children. William Howell, a corporal in Company D, left behind ten children when he enlisted, as did Philip Howard Thomas of Company K and Daniel Stephens of Company C. The largest known family belonged to J. H. Langford of Upson County. When the forty-six-year-old Langford left home to join Company G as a private, he had already sired twelve children.[13]

A greater number of men were neither husbands nor fathers. Two-hundred sixty-one were single in 1860, living with their parents, siblings, or other relatives.[14] Most bachelors in the 66th

---

[10]Again, this counts only inexperienced men.

[11]Noe, *Reluctant Rebels*, 8–9.

[12]"Almost exactly half of [sampled later–enlisting Confederates]…were married," Ibid., 15.

[13]Eighth Census, 1860, Georgia, Free inhabitants, Newton, Pike, Upson, and Walton counties.

[14]Companies A and D of the 16th Georgia Infantry, an early–war regiment, had comparable demographics: "Heads of households constituted 40.1 percent,

Georgia were adolescents and men in their early twenties, though there were a few older bachelors as well. Gabriel Piper and Flavius Lavenby, both forty and both in Company C, were still living, unmarried, at their childhood homes in Newton County until they joined the regiment.[15]

Forty-three men in the group lived neither with family nor with relatives. Some were apprentices, like Henry Rector of Company E, a twenty-nine-year-old millwright in Cass County residing with an older, master millwright. Others were pooling their resources; twenty-three-year-old James Moore of Company B, a clerk from Muscogee County with $100 to his name, lived with three other clerks in Columbus. Still others would eventually become family men. Company B's Madison Darden of Warren County, thirty-seven years old, worked as a farm laborer for an elderly woman named Mrs. Wynn. Darden already owned $3700 in personal property, and after surviving the war he would gain again: Mrs. Wynn's granddaughter, Mary, would become Darden's wife.[16]

More than half of men living apart from family were probably tenants. Thirteen were farmers, farmhands or day laborers, and another eight without listed occupations lived with farm families. Again, their ages varied widely. Brothers William and Jesse Champion were in their teens and worked separately on two Greene County farms. William Taylor of Company A, was twice as old as the Champion brothers but had no more money than

---

dependent sons accounted for 55.2 percent, and single men and tenants 2.2 percent," David G. Smith, "Georgians Seem to Suffer More Than Any Troops in the Service": A Profile of Two Companies of Madison County Confederates," *The Georgia Historical Quarterly*, vol. 79, No. 1 (Spring, 1995) 172.

[15]Eighth Census. 1860, Georgia, Free inhabitants, Newton County.

[16]Ibid., Bartow, Muscogee and Warren counties; Ninth Census, 1870, Georgia, Warren County.

they did. Economic necessity probably forced the Bibb County farmhand to live with James M. Gates, himself a thirty-five-year-old married farmer and father of five.[17]

Whether married or single, living with family, friends or strangers, the soldiers of the 66th Georgia were largely working men. Three-hundred fifty-seven (69 percent of the group) had some occupation listed in the census records. More than fifty different occupations were represented. At least two men worked two or more different kinds of jobs to make a living; the rest were committed to a single line of work.

Given the dominance of agriculture in the antebellum South, it is not surprising that most of Nisbet's soldiers worked the land. Two-hundred eleven, roughly 40 percent of the total group (and 58 percent of all workers) were farmers. Twenty-two more, 6 percent of the men with known occupations, were overseers. Another twenty-one were farmhands, and seven were planters. One man was listed as a sharecropper and another as a tenant. Altogether, 263 men (50 percent of the total group and 72 percent of all workers) were known to have farmed.

They were not the only ones. A closer look at those who claimed no occupation reveals that 101 (19 percent of the total group) lived with farmers, farmhands, or planters. Most of these men were probably doing the same kinds of work. Therefore, at least 364 men in the 66th Georgia—70 percent of the men found in the census—toiled in the fields before figuratively beating their plowshares into swords in 1863.[18]

---

[17]Ibid., Bibb and Green counties.

[18]Similarly, close to 75 percent of the men of Companies A and D, Sixteenth Georgia, had worked as farmers, as had 74 percent of Noe's sampled later-enlisting Confederates. Smith, "Georgians Seem to Suffer," 171, 173; Noe, *Reluctant Rebels,* 17.

Eighty-one farmers who served in the 66th Georgia appear in the agricultural census records. Combined, they tended 5,619 improved acres of land and owned another 8,979 unimproved acres. Their lands were worth a combined $114,690, while their farming implements were worth a total of more than $6,000. In land owned, Reuben Strozier of Greene County might be considered a "typical" farmer. His 80 improved acres and 180 unimproved acres of farmland were worth $2,500, enough for Reuben to ensure a moderately comfortable lifestyle for his wife and six children. John Odell of Hall County owned even more; with over 1,200 acres, worth about $7,000, he was the largest landowner and the second-wealthiest farmer in the group.[19] Sixty-three farmers owned at least some farmland. Nineteen others, though listed as independent farmers in the census records, owned no land according to the agricultural census, and had little else besides. They may have been tenants or hired hands, whose security depended on what they could produce in livestock, fruits, and homemade goods. Most landless farmers in the group had at least something to show for their work; the average value of their products was close to $250. But for every farmer like John Head of Morgan County, who had almost $800 worth of agricultural products, there were several others less industrious or simply less lucky, such as John Kimble. Married with three children, forty-eight-year-old Kimble was in an unenviable position: he owned only $20 worth of livestock (perhaps an old, worn-out mule?) and a mere $8 worth of animals slaughtered.[20] One wonders how Kimble and his family managed to survive.

Even if a farmer in the 66th Georgia had no land, he was likely to own at least one horse, one mule, and two oxen. Many also held

---

[19]Eighth Census, 1860, Manuscript Returns of Productions of Agriculture, Georgia, Greene and Hall counties.

[20]Ibid., Morgan and Taylor counties.

sheep and pigs, averaging one dozen of the former and two dozen of the latter. They planted wheat, rice, oats, rye, peas, beans, barley, and buckwheat, and they cultivated cheese, beeswax, and honey. Mainly, however, they produced three commodities: corn (average, 320 bushels), sweet potatoes (average, 94 bushels), and butter (average, 132 pounds). Though not rich, these farmers made enough in 1860 to get by and to have enough to eat most of the time. Then the war came, and Georgia's farmers suffered greatly. Escalating prices and runaway Confederate inflation kept farmers from buying feed or livestock or replacing worn-out plows and other tools. Impressments and tax-in-kind, which allowed the Confederate government to claim a large part of their produce, hit farmers especially hard. After two years of war, many of Georgia's farmers had become as destitute as John Kimble.

Farmhands in the 66th Georgia were usually somewhat younger than farmers: eleven of the 21 farmhands were 25 years old or younger, while 182 of 211 farmers were at least 30 years old. Not all farmhands were young men though. Benjamin Hardy, John Jones and Sanford Owens were all at least forty years old when they became soldiers. None of these three hands held any more than $150 in total assets.[21]

Like farmers, the overseers who joined the 66th Georgia tended to be older men; fourteen of the twenty-two were at least thirty years old when the war began. In the antebellum South, older men were thought to be better overseers, more responsible at overseeing field work and more capable of physically cowing unruly male slaves. R. B. Perry, a thirty-year-old who became a private in Company E, must have done fairly well at the job, for he enjoyed assets worth almost $6,000. On smaller farms, an overseer's youth was not as great an issue. Well before he turned twenty,

---

[21]Ibid., Bibb, Gordon and Jackson counties.

Lieutenant Ellis Harrison Hull of Company A managed at least one slave on a Screven County farm.[22]

Some men in the 66th Georgia undoubtedly aspired to become planters (landowners with at least twenty slaves). Though sometimes resented by their lower-class neighbors, planters tended to enjoy substantial wealth, power, and prestige. The idealized Southern planter commanded a family, many servants, and a handsome estate, not to mention the affairs of his community.

Half of the men from the 66th Georgia listed as planters met the criteria for their class, at least in terms of relative wealth. James Knox of Company B, William Bush of Company D, and Edward Byrd of Company F each had over $10,000 in assets when the war began. John Chance of Company B might well have been a richer man at an earlier time, though by 1860 the fifty-year-old Burke County native's estate was worth only $1,550. Some Southern men, though, were listed as planters despite their meager holdings. Jesse Tennyson of Company A was such a man; a mere $500 in property hardly qualified the thirty-three-year old resident of Richmond County for the aristocracy, even in his small hometown, Allen Station.[23]

Tenants and sharecroppers like Samuel Reynolds and William Williams tended to own little or nothing. Thirty-one-year-old Williams, who served as a private in Company B, at least had a father with a $6,398 estate, though Williams had to share it with nine siblings. Thirty-nine-year-old Reynolds, on the other hand, had six mouths to feed besides his own and no other family members to help him financially. By joining Company K, Reynolds at least had some income, but if he suffered death or crippling wounds, his family would face hard times.[24]

---

[22]Ibid., Marion and Screven counties.
[23]Ibid., Burke, Columbia, Early and Richmond counties.
[24] Ibid., Paulding and Walton counties.

Agriculture was not the only way that the soldiers of the 66th Georgia had made a living before the war. At least seventy-nine men in the regiment (roughly 22 percent of the workers) claimed some other type of job.[25] After farmwork, mercantilism was the most common occupation, employing thirteen (a little more than 2 percent of all workers). These were prosperous men; with one exception—forty-year-old Henry Snellings of Morgan County— all of them owned property, and their estates tended to be substantial, averaging at least $9,900. A. C. Patman of Company I, for example, had $20,000 in personal property when he became one of Nisbet's lieutenants. Overall, merchants were an older group (nine of them were at least thirty-five years old), mostly family men (ten were married, while nine also had children), and, as with Patman, they tended to become officers (six altogether).[26]

Eleven men (another 2 percent of workers) were laborers. As with farmers, the laborers of the 66th Georgia came in all ages, from nineteen-year-old Augustus Hobbs of Company D to forty-one-year-old Charles McCoy of Company A. Unlike the regiment's merchants, all laborers in the group were poor, enlisted men. Ten owned no property whatsoever, and all remained privates throughout their service. Due perhaps to their lack of material wealth, only three had started families before the war.[27]

Eight men made a living from carpentry. They were somewhat older than the regimental average, with a median age of thirty-seven. They were also family men, most being married with at least two children each. In both wealth and military status, carpenters occupied a rough middle ground between merchants

---

[25] By way of comparison, as many as one-third of Noe's sampled later-enlisting Confederates were not farmers (*Reluctant Rebels*, 17).

[26] Eighth Census, 1860, Georgia, Free inhabitants, Clarke and Morgan counties.

[27] Ibid., Bibb and Stewart counties.

and laborers. Though none of them owned more than $970, at least two-thirds owned something, and while none gained an officer's commission, a few rose higher than private. Jesse Stinson entered the regiment as a sergeant of Company D; Edwin Bernhard gained a corporal's position in Company F; and Hiram Shaver became a corporal in Company H.[28]

For ambitious young Southern men, clerking was sometimes a springboard into a good career. Six men in the regiment, all under the age of thirty, worked as clerks. Like James B. Moore, mentioned earlier, most were single men living apart from family. Two had done fairly well before the war: twenty-seven-year-old Cecil Hammock, the regimental quartermaster, had a $4,500 estate, while Thomas Paine, twenty-four years old, had $3,000. On the whole, however, clerking offered even less money than carpentry.[29]

When war came in 1861, many Southern boys had left school to fight, and quite a few of their teachers had joined up as well. Thereafter education in Georgia, as in other Confederate states, had become sporadic. A number of schools had soon closed for lack of staff, attendance, and tuition.[30] Most likely, James Hailey, John Champion and William Lawrence, the three students in the group, had set aside their studies and returned home before Colonel Nisbet called for recruits. All three boys probably enjoyed somewhat comfortable lives, as their parents each owned at least $10,000 in property. Columbus Alford, a medical student, was in another class altogether; he owned no property and lived in a

---

[28] CSRs for Stinson, Edwin M. Bernard, and Hiram Shaver.
[29] Eighth census, 1860, Georgia, Free inhabitants, Oglethorpe and Thomas counties.
[30] T. Conn Bryan, *Confederate Georgia* (Athens: University of Georgia Press, 1953) 216–29.

boardinghouse in Augusta.[31] For Southern teachers, money could be tight. While two teachers in the group—Moses Brown and Ascon Moody—had wealthy friends and families, a third, Isaac Evans, was not so fortunate. Evans had only about $1,100 in 1860, and he stood to make little more by quitting an exempted profession to become a soldier.[32] What led Evans into the ranks of Company B? Did his school close, ending his exemption? Was he anxious to prove himself a man, to escape the taunts of peers for not enlisting earlier? Did ultra-patriotic neighborhood roughs threaten to harm Evans unless he fought for the Confederacy? Or did an unscrupulous conscript officer force him into the army at gunpoint? We will probably never know.

Millers were also legally exempt from Confederate conscription.[33] Even so, whether from abuses in the system or from some sense of duty, four millers ended up in the 66th Georgia. On the fringes of poverty, their total combined assets amounted to a mere $400 in personal property and not one cent in real property. War further tried this class of workers: Jourdan Bridges deserted, Samuel Music died during the Atlanta Campaign, and Wiley Evans and George Shirley ended their military services in the hospital.[34]

---

[31] Eight census, 1860, Georgia, Free inhabitants, Elbert, Greene, Richmond and Screven counties.

[32] Ibid., Alabama, Free inhabitants, Calhoun County. The First Conscription Act of April, 1862, had exempted teachers with twenty or more pupils. Soon afterwards, the number of teachers ballooned in many parts of the Confederacy. Albert Burton Moore, *Conscription and Conflict in the Confederacy* (New York: Macmillan Co., 1924) 52–55.

[33] Millers were exempted in the Second Conscription Act of October 1862 (Moore, *Conscription and Conflict*, 67–68).

[34] CSRs for Jourdan Bridges, Samuel D. Music, Wiley G. Evans, and George B. Shirley.

In addition to agriculture, millinery, mercantilism, labor, carpentry, clerical work, and education, the men of the 66th Georgia held other skilled and unskilled jobs. A few were tailors (four men each); a few others were grocers (three men each). Two men worked cutting stone, and another two were mechanics. Twenty-four other occupations employed a single man each.[35]

We should also examine how much property the average soldier in the 66th Georgia possessed. Simply dividing total listed assets ($920,215) by the number of men in the group would yield a modest $1,766 per man. In reality, wealth in the 66th Georgia was dispersed unevenly. At least 258 (almost half of the group) were known to be penniless (See table 1). Presumably so were one-half to two-thirds of the rest of the men in the roster, as those not found in the census were often impoverished. Therefore, close to three-quarters of the men of the 66th Georgia (between 500 and 800 out of 1,021) were probably poor.[36] Very few men in the regiment owned any property. Eighty-one men had assets worth between $7 and $499, with an average of $174. Thirty-one men owned between $500 and $999. Surprisingly, seventy-seven men, almost as many as those in the lowest asset bracket, had estates worth between $1,000–4,999. As total wealth exceeded $5,000, the numbers steadily diminished, from twenty-nine men owning

---

[35] These include barber, brick molder, cabinet maker, carriage maker, copper smith, dentist, ditch digger, dress maker, drummer (a traveling salesman) lawyer, literary, machinist, manager, map seller, painter, physician, quarry man, railroad baggage agent, sawyer, shoe maker, storekeeper, trader, watchman, and well digger.

[36] Noe estimated that 58 percent of sampled, later-enlisting Confederates owned no property (*Reluctant Rebels,* 15).

$5,000–9,999, to seventeen men owning $10,000–19,999, to a mere three men owning $20,000–29,000.[37]

The three richest soldiers owned more than $30,000. William Wilson of Putnam County, a private in Company F, had $31,947 when the war began, and though listed as a "farmer," probably bore little resemblance to a common man in a log cabin. Newton County native A. Jackson Summers, who became a lieutenant in Company C, was even wealthier, boasting $59,000 in real and personal property. The wealthiest man of all was Richard Harris of Company G. Forty-two years old when he joined the 66th as a private, Harris owned $6,750 in real property and $61,000 in personal property. Sadly for Harris, his considerable wealth provided no protection from the ravages of disease, for he succumbed to chronic dysentery in a Dalton, Georgia, hospital in April 1864.[38]

As already shown in several of the occupations, age was not necessarily an indicator of wealth in the 66th Georgia. No fewer than forty-seven men older than thirty-five were utterly destitute, whereas at least twelve men under twenty-five, by dint of hard work or good fortune, had acquired some property. There is also parental wealth to consider. Twenty-four-year-old Lewis Harwell of Company G, an only child, owned not one cent in property but surely had some access to his father's $67,000 estate. Josiah Adams, a young lieutenant in Company F, was similarly penniless and similarly blessed; his father, merchant B. F. Adams, had assets of $125,000. The greatest of all parental resources were those enjoyed by Briggs Hopson Napier. The twenty-four-year-old

---

[37] Companies A and D of the 16th Georgia had similar percentages of low-income and middle-class men, although with a smaller percentage of men in the $1,000–$4,999 range (Smith, "Georgians Seem to Suffer," 173, 175–76).

[38] Eighth Census, 1860, Georgia, free inhabitants, Morgan, Newton, and Putnam counties; Richard J. Harris CSR.

lieutenant's Bibb County planter father owned $400,000 in property.[39]

Few in the regiment were as fortunate as these men. Seventeen unemployed, penniless men lived with destitute working fathers. Nine more lived with families owning less than $200 in total property. Even those with property-owning parents usually had other dependent siblings to consider. Of all men without occupations living at home, 134 had at least one brother or sister. An average of four siblings per family shared their parents' scant means with the unemployed men of the 66th Georgia. Most unfortunate of all were those without money of their own, living with poverty-stricken parents *and* a large number of brothers and sisters. Miles Bloodworth of Company E in particular was in a pitiful plight. According to the 1850 census, Miles's parents, who did not own any property, had to take care of eleven children. It is doubtful that the next thirteen years saw improvement in the family's finances. Whether conscription or the promise of army pay caused Miles to fight for the Confederacy, he did not last long, deserting in early September, 1863.[40]

---

[39] Eighth Census, 1860, Georgia, free inhabitants, Bibb, Morgan and Putnam counties.

[40] Seventh Census, 1850, Georgia, Free inhabitants, Wilkinson County; Miles E. Bloodworth CSR.

Table 1
Lower Economic Strata of the Sixty-Sixth Georgia Infantry,
By Company[41]

Co.	#of sampled men	#% of sampled men with no property	#/% of sampled men with >$100 in property	#/% of sampled men >$500 property
A	40	28 (70%)	1 (2.5%)	3 (7.5%)
B	45	19 (42%)	4 (8.8%)	10 (22%)
C	62	25 (40%)	1 (1.6%)	7 (11%)
D	42	19 (45%)	2 (4.7%)	10 (23.8)
E	48	26 (54%)	1 (2%)	7 (14%)
F	47	20 (42%)	0 (0%)	7 (14.8%)
G	53	33 (62%)	0 (0%)	1 (1.8%)
H	48	22(45%)	2 (4%)	6 (12.5%)
I	67	35 (52%)	2 (2.9%)	10 (14.9%)
K	58	31 (53%)	4 (6.8%)	5 (8.6%)

Poor Miles might have quit in smoldering resentment against richer comrades and countrymen. Some historians blame wealthy Southern men for the Confederacy's defeat. Having foisted secession and war on an unwilling populace, the argument goes, these aristocrats quickly excused themselves from wartime sacrifices. Safe behind the front lines, they made fortunes on cotton speculation and illegal trading, leaving the Confederacy's plain folk to do all of the fighting and dying. Demoralized and angered by the callous disregard of the elites, the common-class populace eventually gave up, leading to Confederate collapse.[42]

Even well-to-do Southerners who served in the army have not escaped these historians' censures. Wealthy Southerners have been accused of monopolizing the highest positions in the Confederate

---

[41] This does not include the regiment's field and staff.
[42] Williams, Williams, and Carlson, *Plain Folk in a Rich Man's War*, 8–44.

Army, enjoying better pay, better healthcare, better food, and more flexible furloughs. Meanwhile, humble Confederate privates, suffered and died for a pittance—until they realized they had been duped. Raging against a "rich man's war, poor man's fight," Confederate soldiers struck back with spiraling desertions, until the army simply evaporated.[43]

The extent of class tensions in the Confederate Army as a whole has not yet been quantifiably measured, but looking at wealth in the 66th Georgia offers a regimental-level perspective. Thirty-two commissioned officers of the 66th Georgia appeared in the census records. The richest was Summers, mentioned above, who had $59,000 in assets. Almost half of the sampled officers—including Colonel Nisbet, majors Andrews and Hull, three of seven captains, and nine of twenty lieutenants—had no assets whatsoever. This does not mean that Nisbet and his company commanders were poor; on the contrary, they were solidly upper class. With wealthy parents and connections, they were hardly likely to go hungry during the war, or even to have to do without accustomed luxuries (See table 2.). Even so, an officer's commission was not necessarily indicative of financial well-being.[44] Four lieutenants in Nisbet's regiment had struggled to make ends meet before the war in 1860. Daniel O'Rear of Company H, a married thirty-nine-year old, had only $2,300 to cover himself, his wife, and their two children. Twenty-eight-year-old John Terrell of Company C lived with his four brothers and sisters on $1,300. James Hendon of Company K, age forty-two, owned $618 to feed

---

[43] David Williams, *Rich Man's War: Class, Caste, and Confederate Defeat in the Lower Chattahoochee River Valley* (Athens: University of Georgia Press, 1998) 116–50.

[44] Eighth Census, 1860, Gerogia free inhabitants, Newton County. On average, officers studied by Noe owned twice as much property as enlisted men, though the average for the latter was skewed by several wealthy privates (*Reluctant Rebels,* 16).

and clothe a family of three. Even these three situations seemed manageable when compared to the finances of Company A's J. H. Rogers. Rogers had the burden of caring for his wife and eight children on $2,200, without the help of other family members.[45] Another thirteen lieutenants and two captains were not found in the census records; they too are likely to have been poor men.

Table 2
Personal and Parental Wealth of Some Officers of the Sixty-Sixth Georgia Infantry

Name and rank	Personal wealth	Parental wealth
Col. James C. Nisbet	0	$35,000
Lt. Col. Algernon S. Hamilton	$8,500	?
Maj. Robert N. Hull	0	?
Capt. Moses L. Brown	0	$18,774
Capt. Columbus M. Jordan	0	$1,300
Capt. Thomas L. Langston	$8,000	$6,000
Capt. Alexander H. Reid	$300	$52,550
Capt. Jesse Thornton	0	$2,500
Capt. Charles J. Williamson	$10,000	$125,000
Lt. Josiah Adams	0	$125,000
Lt. Thomas J. P. Atkinson	$11,500	?
Lt. Alfred H. Coates	$1,200	$7,600
Lt. Charles W. Gray	0	$115,500
Lt. Benjamin F. Hammock	$1,000	?
Lt. William C. Massey	0	$10,000
Lt. Briggs H. Napier	0	$400,000
Lt. A. C. Patman	$20,000	?
Lt. Wiley H. Quillian	$8,100	?
Lt. Isaac W. Reese	0	$62,500

---

[45] Ibid., Clarke, Franklin, Pike, and Walker counties.

Lt. William R. Ross	0	$153,400
Lt. John O. Rosser	$8,525	?
Lt. Osborne M. Stone	0	$7,500
Lt. A. Jackson Summers	$52,000	?
Lt. John T. Terrell	$1,300	?
Lt. William M. Weaver	0	$66,560

Sources: Census Records for 1850 and 1860

Non-commissioned officers (NCOs) enjoyed few of the privileges of their superiors and suffered many of the same hardships as the men in the ranks. Even so, a sergeant or a corporal had some authority over others. Lower-class men contributed the majority of NCOs in the 66th Georgia. Two-thirds each of thirty-one sergeants and thirty-three corporals owned less than $1,000 in property; at least thirty-two NCOs in the regiment owned nothing at all. In fact, the humble means of most of these NCOs makes the significant wealth of a few all the more conspicuous. Corporal John Odell, mentioned earlier, was in the top 3 percent of wealth in the regiment's sample because he owned $14,505 in property. Doctor Dial of Company H was even wealthier; the Newton County farmer-turned-sergeant had over $22,000 in property—more than was owned by twenty out of twenty-one lieutenants in the group.[46]

With limited capital in the Southern states, slaves were often the only measurable source of antebellum wealth. Eighty men in the 66th Georgia owned slaves, and sixty-two others lived with slave owners, meaning that a little more than one-quarter of the

---

[46] Ibid., Hall and Newton counties. Non-commissioned officers in Noe's study tended to be not only poorer than all sampled officers, but also only half as wealthy as enlisted men (*Reluctant Rebels,* 16).

soldiers in the group were connected to slavery in some way.[47] Slave ownership was most heavily concentrated in Company G, where 13 soldiers claimed 206 of the 642 slaves owned by the regiment's men. Seven men owned twenty or more slaves, which classified them as planters, though they were not noted as such in the census records.[48] Surprisingly, only two of these planters were commissioned officers, though many of the other officers lived with planter-class parents or neighbors. Nine captains and lieutenants owned a combined 103 slaves (one-sixth of the total number), with an average of 11 slaves apiece. In this group, Lieutenant Summers of Company C owned the most at twenty-nine. Thirteen sergeants and corporals owned a combined sixty-six slaves (average, five slaves for each of these NCOs), but the majority of the regiment's slaves belonged to enlisted men. Fifty-eight privates owned a grand total of 473 slaves (average 8 slaves per man), making these soldiers wealthier (in human property, at least) than their squad and platoon commanders and almost as wealthy as their company commanders. In fact, the largest slave owner in the sample was an enlisted man. John Wilkes of Company G, who joined the regiment as a private in August 1863, but was discharged shortly afterwards for deafness, owned fifty slaves, almost one-tenth of all the slaves represented.[49]

However limited, these data suggest that, while the highest

---

[47] Noe found a much greater percentage of Confederate soldiers connected to slavery in his sample—43 percent (*Reluctant Rebels*, 16). Joseph Glatthaar emphasized a similar connection in a demographic sampling of the Army of Northern Virginia in his *General Lee's Army: From Victory to Collapse* (New York: Simon and Schuster, 2008).

[48] Conversely, the "planters" found in the slave census—John Chance, James Knox, William Bush, and Edward Byrd—owned fewer than twenty slaves each.

[49] John A. Wilkes CSR; Eighth Census, 1860, Manuscript Returns of Slaves, Georgia, Newton and Troup counties.

positions in late-war Confederate regiments might have been held by rich men, wealth did not always translate into rank. Sometimes, a man without title, lineage, or assets could become a leader, while a man who had all three might find himself in the ranks taking orders from his social inferiors.[50] In electing their company officers, the men of the 66th Georgia demonstrated a preference for men of means, yet they did not exclude lower-class men. Battle also acted as a social leveler, killing or incapacitating some blue-blooded officers and forcing a few lower-class men to exercise command.[51]

Samplings of early- and late-war soldiers in the Army of Northern Virginia, taken by Joseph Glatthaar, offer a few enlightening comparisons to Nisbet's men. Most of Glathaar's early-war soldiers were younger than those who joined the 66th Georgia, and their median wealth—$1,365 for the "boys of '61" and $1,312 for those who joined in 1862—tended to be greater. Officers in Glatthaar's group were often twice as wealthy as privates, although "those who enlisted in 1862 tended to have a greater concentration of extremes—[either] very wealthy [or] very poor." Counting both soldiers who owned slaves and those living with slave-owning families or friends, Glatthaar concluded that almost 50 percent of the men he examined had some connection to slavery.[52]

Of greater interest to this study are those men in Glatthaar's sample who enlisted in 1863 or later, the same time that the 66th

---

[50] Commenting on Southern aristocrats who complained about serving under lower-born men, Bell I. Wiley concluded that "sensitiveness to class seems to have been voiced more frequently by the rich than by the poor," Wiley, *The Life of Johnny Reb: The Common Soldier of the Confederacy* (Baton Rouge: LSU Press, 1943) 337–39.

[51] Mark V. Wetherington, *Plain Folks' Fight: The Civil War & Reconstruction in Piney Woods Georgia* (Chapel Hill: UNC Press, 2005) 133.

[52] Glatthaar, *General Lee's Army*, 18–21, 203–205.

Georgia was formed. They "tended towards the edges of the age curve," representing teenagers and middle-aged men in almost equal measure. Almost half were married, and their personal and family wealth was greater than those of the 1861 or 1862 soldiers.[53] This suggests that men of means were more likely to join late in Virginia than elsewhere. While the majority of the officers and some of the enlisted men of the 66th might have been rich, most of Nisbet's men were quite poor despite their older average ages.

The soldiers of the 66th Georgia entered Confederate service in one of three ways: volunteering, substituting for others, or being conscripted. In most cases, there is no way to prove which process brought in which men. Using the rough percentages suggested by Noe—48 percent volunteers, 18 percent substitutes, and 34 percent conscripts—would yield an estimate of 248, 93, and 176, respectively, for of the 517 men in the group.[54] The number of substitutes would be the lowest of the three, but the other two percentages are nothing more than guesswork. Personal writings from the men of the 66th do not address how the writers or their comrades became part of the Confederate Army. Nisbet's men might have been mostly volunteers who believed they would stay near home, or who had become convinced that *now* was the time to defend state, nation, and loved ones. On the other hand, long casualty lists, hard times at home, and a deep feeling of war-weariness might just as well have meant that most of them were reluctant Confederates and resistant conscripts.

Thankfully, there is one way to identify some men in the regiment as volunteers. The service records for some of Nisbet's men note that they were due a $50 bounty—the same amount promised to volunteers in Georgia newspaper advertisements—in

---

[53] Ibid., 358–59.
[54] Noe, *Reluctant Rebels*, 2.

summer or fall 1863. Because many Confederate records were lost during the war, and others are incomplete, we cannot know whether the men so noted were the *only* volunteers in the regiment. We can, however, examine the financial and occupational backgrounds of this group.

Of the 1,029 men who served in the 66th Georgia, 174 were due the $50 bounty according to their service records. Ninety-eight appear in the census records, which tell us a few things about these known volunteers. First, they were mostly enlisted men. While sixteen were non-commissioned officers, and one (Richard Richards) was a hospital steward, the rest were mere privates. Second, their ages varied considerably. Thirty known volunteers were younger than twenty-five, and thirty-eight were age forty or older. Third, most came from the particular counties that supplied the bulk of the regiment's manpower, especially Newton, Dekalb, Bibb, and Gwinnett. Fourth, more than half were married men, with an average of four children. Finally, with the exception of two men, they joined one of three companies: C, D, and E. As mentioned earlier, Company C had almost uniform county demographics, suggesting a large, perhaps majority, contingent of volunteers, while Companies D and E, drawing from several dozen counties each, may have had equal mixtures of willing men and conscripts.

Occupationally, the ninety-eight known volunteers were representative of the larger group. Sixty-one were farmers, farmhands, overseers, or planters, and fifteen more lived with farming families. Financially, most were hard-pressed. Forty-four owned less than $100 in property; another eighteen owned less than $500. Poor men like these might be expected to seek extra income, even at the risk of enemy bullets, and even though $50 in

Confederate money could not buy very much in 1863.[55] More surprising is that several known volunteers were wealthy men. Stephen Brown, William Bush, and R. F. G. Roberts each owned more than $10,000 in property. Assuming that they were still solvent, they could have probably paid for a substitute or even bribed a judge to avoid military service. What caused Bush, Brown, and Roberts to volunteer? Given that they were in their 40s, and that Brown and Roberts disappeared after being absent without leave in 1864, it seems plausible that they signed up for the usual reasons, only to discover that army life was quite strenuous for men of their age.[56]

One other volunteer deserves special mention, because he was the only one who seems to have actually received the money. Twenty-nine-year-old Sanford Baty, a bachelor farmer with no property listed in the census, lived in Dekalb County with his widowed mother Gracy and aunt Margaret before joining Broyle's 36th Georgia Infantry in April 1862. Baty and his regiment were sent to Vicksburg, Mississippi, where Baty was detailed as a nurse during the siege (May–July 1863). Captured when the Confederate garrison at Vicksburg surrendered to Northern forces on 4 July, Baty was paroled five days later and returned to Georgia.[57] As with most of the Vicksburg garrison, Baty violated his parole when he joined the 66th Georgia in early September, before he had been properly exchanged. In his new regiment, Baty rose to the rank of sergeant, and served briefly as a brigade quartermaster in late 1863, never wounded, never sick, and never absent during his

---

[55] Though "not all [Confederate bounty soldiers] were poor," Noe found that "most men who enlisted for the bounty money really did need it" (*Reluctant Rebels*, 106–107).

[56] CSRs for Stephen A. Brown, William J. Bush, and R. F. G. Roberts; Eighth Census, 1860, Georgia, Free inhabitants, Early, Newton and Gwinnett counties.

[57] Ibid., Dekalb County; Sanford H. Baty CSR.

time under Nisbet. Baty's location and situation at the end of the war are unknown. He does not seem to have surrendered with his comrades.[58]

Baty's service record shows that he was paid $50 in early fall 1863. Why was Baty the only soldier in the regiment known to have received the money promised to volunteers? It cannot have been due simply to the army taking pity on his poverty; plenty of other known volunteers were just as poor. Nor was Baty the only volunteer living with a widowed mother; so were Lazarus Cannady, Joseph Carmichael, John Henry, Thomas Massengale, and Doctor Osburn. Baty could have claimed that, as a veteran of earlier campaigns, he deserved the bounty, but other men with prior experience, such as Charles Dupree, W. B. Foreman, William Gaulding, William King, and James Peake, never collected their shares.[59] Nisbet's proffered bounty was not the first that Baty had received. Earlier, in his service with the 36th Georgia, Baty had received a similar amount for reenlisting. It is possible that Baty had picked up some sort of inside knowledge about the Confederate bounty system and cleverly worked it to his advantage. However, Jason Dupree, Thomas Leverett, and James Merritt had also received early-war bounties, but were unable to secure the same in Nisbet's regiment.[60] Baty was not related to any of the regiment's officers, and as an NCO, he would not have had any supporters in the Confederate War Department. Maybe Baty was simply lucky when he pocketed more money than other volunteers in the 66th.

Conscripts and substitutes in the 66th Georgia warrant separate demographic analysis. It is difficult, however, to positively identify

---

[58] Baty CSR.
[59] CSRs for Baty, Charles W. Dupree, W. B. Foreman, William D. Gaulding, William D. King, and James S. P. Leake.
[60] CSRs for Baty, Jason L. Dupree, Thomas M. Leverett, and James Merritt.

drafted men. Though a number of men claimed to have been forced into the army, none were classified as conscripts in their service records. Moreover, their claims of unwilling service were generally made under questionable circumstances, as discussed in a later chapter.

Two men are known to have been discharged from the 66th Georgia by finding two substitutes to take their places. Jonathan Burgess of Company K, who joined in August 1863, found a willing replacement within four months and left. Nothing else is known about Burgess, not even the name of the substitute who replaced him. The other man who left was F. J. Wright, a thirty-nine-year-old from Newton County. Wright was married with five children, and owned a respectable $23,730 in real and personal property. He provided a substitute the same day he reported to Macon.[61]

Fifty-one-year-old Daniel Stephens, also of Newton County, was Wright's substitute. Too old for the draft, Stephens worked as a farmer, got married, had ten children, and had accrued a paltry $260 in property before the war. Stephens's situation in 1863 must have been especially dire for him to have left behind a large family and joined the Confederate Army. Promised a $50 bounty, Stephens may have never received it. When Stephens succumbed to severe diarrhea in September 1864, he became simply one more casualty, but his death must have been devastating for his family.[62]

Another substitute joined Company C, although it is not known who he relieved. William Stewart, age twenty-six, married,

---

[61] F. J. Wright CSR; Eighth Census, 1860, Georgia, Free inhabitants, Newton County. "The successful seekers of [Confederate] substitutes were...men with the money required to hire a man in their stead. The substitutes themselves...seem to have been wretchedly poor" (Noe, *Reluctant Rebels*, 120).

[62] Ibid., Newton County; Daniel Stephens CSR.

and, like Stephens, a humble farmer in Newton County, owned about twice as much property—$545 worth, which still wasn't much. Stewart joined the same day as Stephens, was detailed as a provost guard in late summer 1864, and was fatally stricken by pneumonia in February 1865.[63]

In summary, the "typical" soldier of the 66th Georgia Infantry was either a teenager or a thirty-five- to forty-five-year-old farmer from the Plantation Belt. If married, he might have had three or four children and a 64-acre farm; if single, he probably lived with his parents and several siblings on a similarly modest piece of land.[64] His means were small; the odds are that he owned nothing. Assuming that fortune had smiled on him, he might have had a few hundred dollars in property. Perhaps he owned a single slave, though more than he likely would have preferred to borrow one.

Half of Colonel Nisbet's men never appeared in the census records, so we can only guess what their lives were like. Were they older, or young boys? Were they struggling farmers, landless laborers, unemployed professionals? How many were bachelors, and how many were married? Did they have even two cents to rub together?

It is hard to imagine a set of men in humbler circumstances than those described above. By summer 1863, the Confederate Army was scraping the absolute bottom of its manpower barrel. Combat and disease had already claimed tens of thousands of lives. Many of the young, middle- and upper-class early-war volunteers—whose numbers were never great to begin with—were dead. Other able-bodied Southerners had decided to stay out of

---

[63] Ibid., Newton County; William T. Stewart CSR.

[64] For the 212 farmers found in the agricultural census, the average farm was 80 total acres. Here, the number is averaged using all known agricultural workers (263). If divided again by the additional number of agricultural workers estimated above, each man would have had 43 total acres.

the fighting. For the Confederacy to survive, a different type of man had to fill the gaps in the thin, grey lines. Adolescent or middle-aged, his pockets nearly bare, this man made a living by the sweat of his brow, scratching out a bare subsistence on a small swath of sun-baked soil, without much chance to better his station. He was a world apart from Georgians who had joined the Confederate Army in 1861 and 1862, who were on average younger than him and wealthier, with fewer familial concerns. Like them, he would have to face the unforgiving test of battle.

Chapter 4

From Macon to Dalton:
The First Year of Service

Captain Nisbet was not in Georgia when his regiment began to take shape. He spent summer and part of fall 1863 in Richmond, badgering the Confederate War Department to expand his recruiting authority. Nisbet succeeded, for the 66th Georgia included men from all over the state. Tatnall Square in downtown Macon, Nisbet's hometown, became the site of Camp Cooper, the regiment's first home. With Nisbet absent, Captain Hamilton, assisted by Nisbet's brother John, took charge of assembling the 66th Georgia.[1]

Thirty-seven-year-old Edwin McSwain, a bachelor farmer from Tatnall County, was the regiment's first enlisted man, joining on 22 April.[2] Others might have tried to join at the same time, although Nisbet remembered Confederate conscription agents dragging off many of his men in the first few months of recruitment. Another full month passed before Nisbet gained three more permanent soldiers: Sugar Partin, J. J. Price, and G. W. Scarborough, all of whom joined on 23 May. From then on, the regiment grew apace. Thirty men entered the ranks in June, 141 in July, 396 in August, and 294 in September. By October,

---

[1] James C. Nisbet, *Four Years on the Firing Line* (Chattanooga TN: Imperial Press, 1911) 191–95.

[2] Eighth Census, 1860, Georgia, free inhabitants, Tatnall County; Edwin McSwain compiled service record (CSR), National Archives and Records Administration (NARA), Washington, DC (All CSR citations are for the 66th Georgia Infantry unless otherwise noted.).

the regiment was almost at full strength: Company H had 97 men, and seven other companies at least 80 men each.[3]

No sooner had they joined or been forced into the regiment than a few men decided to leave. Twenty-seven enlisted men, almost half of them from Company A, deserted the 66th Georgia during summer and early fall 1863. William Jackson Pirkle claimed that, as an ordained Baptist minister, he was exempt from military service, and left the very day after his induction.[4] William Walden entered the ranks on 16 August and likewise took "French leave" within twenty-four hours.[5] H. K. Crumpler and William Mullice both deserted after two days of military service.[6] William Cosgrove, Elijah Evans, G. E. Peacock, William Taylor and W. T. Ward lasted about a week.[7] The other deserters served between two weeks and one month before leaving. Not all of the regiment's first deserters left for good. George Chandler and John Powell, both of Company C, deserted on the same day (17 August) and reappeared on the same day (1 November).[8] The two may have decided to leave together and then to return. Whether a sense of duty or the fear of punishment motivated them none can say, although only one recaptured deserter from the 66th Georgia was known to have been executed.

Thirteen early deserters can be found in the census records. The majority of them were single men in their late thirties; four

---

[3] This summary of the growth of the regiment is drawn from the regimental roster in Henderson, *Roster*, vol. 6, 693–771. At full strength, an infantry company numbered 100 officers and men.

[4] William J. Pirkle CSR. Pirkle's listed occupation was "map seller" (Eighth Census, 1860, Georgia, free inhabitants, Hall County).

[5] William Walden CSR.

[6] CSRs for H. K. Crumpler and William Mullice.

[7] CSRs for William Cosgrove, Elijah Evans, G. E. Peacock, and William Taylor.

[8] CSRs for George W. Chandler and John A. Powell.

were fathers. Aside from erstwhile minister Pirkle, who owned $3,300 in assets, they were a lower-class group, with nine owning no property at all. One of the deserters, William Tharpe, was a known volunteer. The son of a middle-class planter, Tharpe might have been upset at not immediately receiving the promised bounty, for he left camp nine days after joining Nisbet's regiment. Tharpe went on to serve in the 27th Georgia for the next several months, then finally returned to the 66th in March 1864, and was never punished for his absence.[9]

Desertion accounted for most of the regiment's initial attrition, whereas death claimed a mere four men during the long, hot summer of 1863. In Company B, penniless thirty-three-year-old Private Josiah Raimey of Rabun County succumbed to an unknown malady in early August. Sometime in the following weeks, Privates W. J. Johnson, A. Morgan, and G. W. Street of Company G also passed away.[10] Although a large percentage of Nisbet's men were older than the average Confederate soldier, the regiment's death toll during its formation was surprisingly low.

The 66th Georgia continued to grow, and it was not long before Nisbet found that his regiment had become oversized. Infantry regiments in Confederate service were limited to ten companies, comprising 1,000 officers and men. As volunteers and draftees continued to pour into Camp Cooper, more than compensating for the few men who had died or deserted, the regiment reached its peak strength (on paper): 1,265 officers and

---

[9] Seventh Census, 1850, Georgia, free inhabitants, Troup County; William Tharpe CSR.

[10] Eighth Census, 1860, Georgia, free inhabitants, Rabun County; CSRs for W. J. Johnson, A. Morgan, Josiah Raimey, and G. W. Street. Johnson, Morgan, and Street do not have specified dates of death. Because they all joined on the same day, because they were listed as having died in Macon, and because their records are otherwise very slim, it seems likely that all three died during this time period.

men, divided into 13 companies.[11] Early in the war, Confederate officials had accepted regiments that had slightly more men than the legal limit. In every such regiment, campaign attrition swiftly reduced surplus manpower. Nisbet's regiment was different; it was far larger than the Confederate War Department would allow, and attrition had scarcely slowed its growth. Even if there were no legal issues, prudence necessitated a reorganization of the regiment. Otherwise, the 66th Georgia would be too large to supply and equip, and too cumbersome to maneuver in combat.

Nisbet took credit for solving this problem. With Richmond's permission, he split off the three extra companies to form a separate unit. The resulting new unit, the 26th Georgia Infantry Battalion, served alongside the 66th for a time. Nisbet's brother, John, a veteran of the 2nd Georgia Infantry Battalion, commanded the battalion.[12]

While Hamilton and John Nisbet were still busy gathering recruits and conscripts, the 66th Georgia began its active service. In spring 1863, the Confederate War Department had grown concerned about Federal forces menacing coastal Florida. The day before Nisbet's recruiting advertisements appeared in Georgia newspapers, Secretary of War Seddon notified General Howell Cobb of a major enemy movement in Cobb's department, and urged Cobb to reinforce General Joseph Finnegan, the Confederate commander in Florida. Sometime in August 1863, while Nisbet was still in Richmond, Cobb ordered the 66th Georgia to head south. Because the regiment had not completed

---

[11] Lillian Henderson lists 1,021 men who joined the 66th Georgia Infantry, *Roster*, vol. 6, 693–771; the 26th Georgia Battalion had at least 244 men (Janet B. Hewitt, *Georgia Confederate Soldiers, 1861–1865*, vol. 4 [Wilmington NC: Broadfoot Publishing Co., 1998] 559–60).

[12] Nisbet, *Four Years*, 194–95; John W. Nisbet CSR.

its organization, Captain Hamilton selected four companies, formed them into a battalion, and left for Florida.[13]

Two of those who journeyed to Florida were Private William Rabun Hurst of Company C and his brother James. They had both entered the 66th Georgia in early August, although neither man wanted to be in the regiment—James was anxious for non-combat duty, while William preferred to pay a substitute and go back home. After (one imagines) some haggling with their company commander Captain Parks, James and William left Camp Cooper in order to visit a man who had offered to take William's place. General Cobb's summons arrived while the Hurst brothers were out on this business, and when they returned, disappointed, to Macon—the substitute had opted out at the last minute, despite the promise of $3,500—their comrades were gone. Rather than desert, the Hurst brothers dutifully left by train and stagecoach for Florida, though they took their time getting there.[14]

Upon reaching Florida, Hamilton's battalion was stationed at Quincy, a hamlet near Tallahassee, in a cantonment named for Lamar Cobb, General Cobb's son. The camp, described by William Hurst as "an old field tolerably convenient to a very bold

---

[13] James A. Seddon to Howell Cobb, 23 March 1863, Telegrams Sent by the Confederate Secretary of War, NARA; US War Department, *The War of the Rebellion: A Compilation of the Official Records of the Union and Confederate Armies* (Washington, DC: US Government Printing Office, 1880–1901) vol. 28, pt. 2, p. 328 (Hereafter cited as *OR*; all citations are from series 1 unless otherwise noted.). A close look at the regiment's CSRs suggests that companies A through D were the first to be transferred to Florida.

[14] William R. Hurst to wife, 28 August 1863, Hurst Papers, Kennesaw Mountain National Battlefield Park (KMNBP). Hurst was in good company: "Thirty-six [sampled later-enlisting Confederate soldiers], 11.25 percent of the total, contemplated hiring a substitute at some point" (Kenneth W. Noe, *Reluctant Rebels: The Confederates who Joined the Army after 1861* [Chapel Hill: University of North Carolina Press, 2010] 114–15).

spring…in a very level piny [sic] woods country," also housed the 64th Georgia Infantry and the 5th Florida Cavalry Battalion. Eventually, the rest of the regiment and the 26th Georgia Battalion arrived at Camp Cobb.[15]

The 66th Georgia spent almost two months in Camp Cobb, never coming within sight of a Yankee soldier. Its assignment was to serve as the garrison of Quincy. When not guarding the public buildings in town—a duty that William Hurst considered "very tiresome"—Nisbet's men kept busy building warmer barracks, spurred on by an unseasonable cold snap.[16]

For William Hurst, Camp Cobb was "not to be compared with home." He missed his family and grumbled about the cold nights, ramshackle dwellings, and bad rations at Quincy. Hurst again considered hiring a substitute, but was afraid that leaving Confederate service would only make him liable to state conscription. Deciding that his wife needed the substitute money more than he did, he encouraged her to buy more land or hire extra field hands. Hurst felt even lonelier when his brother James suddenly took an unauthorized leave of absence. He dreamed nightly of coming back to Georgia and wept bitter tears over each letter from home. Though his reassurances to family sometimes rang hollow ("I am in as good spirit as you could expect under the circumstances"), Hurst grimly soldiered on.[17]

---

[15] Hurst to wife, 28 August 1863, Hurst Papers; Nisbet, *Four Years*, 195–96; "Soldiers Cemetery in Eastern Cemetery, Quincy, Florida," http://pone.com/ts/EasternCemetery001.htm.

[16] Ibid.; William R. Ross to sister, 15 September 1863, Napier-Blackman-Ross-Rose (NBRR) Collection, Middle Georgia Archives. In early September, Hamilton requested a froe (an axe with a wedge-shaped blade) "for the purpose of getting boards to cover shelters for the men, not having any tents" (unfiled item, Hamilton CSR).

[17] Hurst to wife, 28 August, 11 and 22 September 1863, Hurst Papers. Hurst's pessimism about escaping military service was well-founded, for "while

Lieutenant William Ross, by contrast, had a good time in Florida. Rank has its privileges, of course, and Ross availed himself of them. At Camp Cobb, Ross was mainly responsible for supervising the construction of barracks and filing reports. These duties, which Ross claimed kept him from writing home more often, were not enough to keep him from taking in the local social scene. The lieutenant attended several parties, shamelessly flirting with Floridian belles whom he considered "pretty fast." Things nearly went awry at one get-together when a familiar lady friend confronted Ross about his engagement to a Georgia girl, but "of course I feigned ignorance as to the fact, and…left her under the impression that the report was false." As a frequent dinner guest of local citizens, Ross also ate very well, much better than his men. One elaborate dinner featured "bacon and greens[,] turkey… chicken fried, beef tongue, sausage…potatoes fried[,] corn and vegetables of all kinds…chikin [sic] pie…and butter," followed by "pound cake…with sauce…preserved peaches, pears and watermelon rind" and washed down with "some of the best wine I ever drank." Ross blamed the ladies for stuffing him, but he "did not know when I would ever have such another chance and thought I had better make the best of that one." With a sigh of contentment, Ross told his sister: "I am well pleased with this country and grow more and more so."[18]

Soon enough, the regiment's time at Camp Cobb came to an end. In October 1863, the 66th Georgia was ordered to leave Florida for duty further north. Nisbet, who finally reached the regiment about this time, wrote that Hamilton had begged him to send the 66th to "active service in the field; or that the troops…be

---

thirty-three [sampled] men sought substitutes…only four were successful…[and] many of the successful…ended up back in uniform whatever their cash outlay for a substitute" (Noe, *Reluctant Rebels*, 120).

[18] Ross to sister, 15 September 1863, NBRR Collection.

sent to one of the principal armies." Otherwise malaria from the Florida swamps, which Hamilton claimed was raging through the camps, might put the entire regiment out of commission.[19]

Statistics gleaned from the regiment's roster do not bear out this explanation. Attrition within the 66th Georgia during its time in Florida was low. Five men in the regiment died at Camp Cobb: three from unknown causes, one from sickness, and one—the unfortunate Private Joseph "Dock" Osborne—of a freak lightning strike. Twenty-one other men were listed in hospitals during their stay in Florida, suffering mostly from "fever," but also from "debility" and, in the case of thirty-year-old Private Philip McIntyre, "want of stamina." W. D. King of Company E had a three month bout of rheumatism that forced him to go home and recuperate. One officer, Lieutenant J. M. Rasberry, resigned due to a severe hernia. Eight men deserted, maybe before they even reached Florida. J. D. Allen and Thompson Townes, probably conscripts, were sued out of the regiment by writ of habeas corpus. All told, the regiment lost a mere 3 percent of its strength in the "piny woods" near Quincy. It had hardly been decimated by the environs.[20]

More likely reasons for the transfer were Nisbet's intentions and the course of the war. Nisbet was now in command of a full regiment, but this was not enough. Young and ambitious, he felt powerfully drawn to the battlefield, and his previous combat experiences probably whetted his appetite for glory and renown. Having accomplished so much at such a young age, Nisbet would not have been content to spend the rest of his army career guarding a quiet little town in Florida. Nisbet wanted to fight, and

---

[19] Nisbet, *Four Years*, 195–96.
[20] See CSRs for J. D. Allen, W. D. King, Philip McIntyre, Joseph H. Osborne, J. M. Rasberry, and Thompson P. Townes.

when it became clear that he would not have the chance to do so at Quincy, he sought another theater of operations.

Conveniently for Nisbet, he and his men were desperately needed elsewhere. Fall 1863 found the Confederacy in a bad situation. In the east, Robert E. Lee's Army of Northern Virginia had encountered the Union army of the Potomac near Gettysburg, in early July, and attacked it, only to suffer a devastating defeat. In the west, Confederates at Vicksburg had surrendered to Northern forces under General Ulysses S. Grant, followed a week later by the garrison at Port Hudson. Even as Nisbet's 1,200 volunteers and conscripts poured into the streets of Macon, more than 52,000 of their comrades were being laid in shallow graves, nursed in hospitals, or marched off to prison camps.[21]

Hard on the heels of these twin disasters came word that the Army of Tennessee had been outmaneuvered and forced to abandon most of Tennessee. Chattanooga, a key river and railway junction town near the north Georgia border, was now endangered by the Union Army of the Cumberland. If the Army of Tennessee lost Chattanooga, Georgia would be exposed to invasion. Hastily, the Confederate War Department began reinforcing General Bragg's army with units from Mississippi, the Carolinas, and Virginia.[22] General Cobb was also asked to send troops, and he promptly released 2,500 men for duty with the

---

[21] Confederate losses were about 22,000 at Gettysburg and about 30,000 at Vicksburg (Noah Anne Trudeau, *Gettysburg: A Testing of Courage* [New York: Harper Collins Publishers, 2001] 529); Michael B. Ballard, *Vicksburg: The Campaign that Opened the Mississippi* (Chapel Hill: University of North Carolina Press, 2004) 398.

[22] Steven Woodworth, *Six Armies in Tennessee: The Chickamauga and Chattanooga Campaign* (Lincoln: University of Nebraska Press, 1998) 1–46.

Army of Tennessee in early September.[23] Shortly afterwards, Cobb sent off the 66th Georgia.

Shortages of transportation slowed the regiment's transfer north, during which time the Army of Tennessee evacuated Chattanooga and retreated into northern Georgia. Bolstered by reinforcements, the Confederates turned and confronted the Army of the Cumberland along the banks of Chickamauga Creek (18–20 September 1863). At the end of the fighting, the Army of Tennessee won the field, albeit at a loss of 18,000 irreplaceable veterans. Chickamauga proved to be a pyrrhic victory for the Confederacy, for the Union army simply retreated into the fortifications of Chattanooga.[24]

On the final day of the battle, Nisbet's men began to arrive in Atlanta, Georgia. They spent a month in the city, guarding Northern prisoners taken at Chickamauga and waiting for the rest of regiment to trickle in from Florida. Sergeant James Crane of Company K, the seventeen-year-old son of an upper-middle-class Athens brick mason, was one of the last to leave Quincy. Crane resented having to abandon his Camp Cobb shanty, which he had almost finished, and his mood did not improve when his company was forced to march through the rain to reach Atlanta. Nisbet, too, was irritated, having been sidelined from combat once again. Lieutenant Ross, on the other hand, was thankful to have missed Chickamauga.[25]

---

[23] Cobb to Samuel Cooper, 28 September 1863, Telegrams Sent to the Confederate Secretary of War, NARA.

[24] See Woodworth, *Six Armies*, 47–128. Though he was not a participant, Nisbet later wrote extensively about the battle (*Four Years*, 201–35).

[25] Nisbet, *Four Years*, 196–97; Eighth Census, 1860, Georgia, free inhabitants, Clarke County; James P. Crane to father, 18 October 1863, Crane letters, Atlanta History Center; Ross to sister, 15 September 1863, BNRR Collection. After the war, adjutant William LeConte somehow remembered

While the 66th Georgia waited in Atlanta, it received a much-
needed shipment of clothing. General A. R. Lawton, the Georgia
quartermaster general, had urged Richmond on 14 October to
supply Nisbet's men with 194 pairs of pants, 194 jackets, 194
pairs of drawers, 194 shirts, 194 pairs of socks, 194 forage caps,
and one pair of shoes for every man. "The men are without the
things named," Nisbet told his superiors, and "cannot draw them
at this post." More than two weeks passed with no answer, but on
29 October, sixteen boxes, containing all the requested items,
arrived at Columbus, Georgia, and were shipped east.[26] At length,
transportation snarls were untangled and the 66th Georgia moved
again. A short train ride took the regiment up the Western &
Atlantic Railroad to Chickamauga Station, Tennessee, about 5
miles west of Chattanooga and in the rear of the Army of
Tennessee. Nisbet's men arrived at the station in late October or
early November, debarked, and marched off to the valley of
Chattanooga Creek, on the left center of the army. The 66th
Georgia, along with the 26th Georgia Battalion, was then assigned
to the brigade of Brigadier General Claudius C. Wilson, a mostly
Georgian organization that had sustained heavy losses at
Chickamauga. Wilson's Brigade, in turn, belonged to the division
of Major General William H. T. Walker, which was part of the
corps of Lieutenant General William J. Hardee.[27]

---

that the 66th Georgia had fought at Chickamauga and been "badly cut up and
decimated" ("Events of My Life," 20).

[26] A. R. Lawton to Richmond, 14 October 1863, Nisbet CSR; Nisbet to
Richmond, 29 October 1863, Nisbet CSR.

[27] Uncertainty surrounds the exact date when the 66th Georgia joined the
Army of Tennessee. Nisbet said that his regiment reached Chickamauga
Station on 21 October (*Four Years*, 196–97), although the army's Special
Orders 294 (12 November) noted that the 66th was "now en route" (*OR*, vol.
31, pt. 3, pp. 685–86).

Nisbet later offered an amusing anecdote about the Chattanooga Campaign to illustrate the inexperience of his men. While on its way to an inspection by General Hardee, the 66th Georgia passed behind the veteran division of General Benjamin Franklin Cheatham. Cheatham's soldiers, aroused by the sound of Nisbet's column marching by, came out to watch the rubes. Noticing that the 66th Georgia had far more men than a standard regiment, Cheatham's men sarcastically asked, "What brigade is that?" Nisbet's men, hearing the query, and not yet realizing that Confederate brigades were designated by the name of the brigade commander, responded with the regimental number. This provoked plenty of laughs from the veterans. "That bloody old 66th brigade…is a whopper!" Cheatham's men chortled.[28]

Almost as soon as he and his men had settled into camp, Nisbet was made aware of two things. The first was his own promotion to brigade command. General Wilson had been laid low by "camp fever," an affliction which sent him to his grave in late November. Because many of Wilson's regimental officers had been killed or wounded at Chickamauga, Nisbet was the senior officer in the brigade. Four months after resigning his captaincy in the 21st Georgia, Nisbet held temporary command of almost 2,000 soldiers.[29]

The second thing that Nisbet learned was that the Army of Tennessee was in turmoil. A score of its generals and probably the better part of its officers and enlisted men were disgusted, demoralized, and afraid that their next battle would prove to be a disaster. Much of the discontent stemmed from the army's

---

[28] Nisbet, *Four Years*, 197–98.

[29] Ezra J. Warner, *Generals in Gray: Lives of the Confederate Commanders* (Baton Rouge: Louisiana State University Press, 1959) 339; Nisbet, *Four Years*, 198. Nisbet's promotion to colonel, as well as most of the officer commissions in the regiment, dated from 24 October 1863.

contentious and cantankerous commander General Braxton Bragg. Chronically ill and ill-tempered, Bragg was a superb administrator and a bold planner who tended to choke under pressure. His sixteen-month tenure in command of the army had been characterized by command-level infighting, organizational confusion, and squandered strategic opportunities. Bragg's biggest problem was that he had plenty of enemies, both in and out of the army, who blamed him for all of the Confederacy's reverses in the western theater. Even the victory at Chickamauga had not dampened criticism of Bragg. Many of his subordinates argued that he ought to have destroyed the Union army in that battle, rather than merely driven it back to Chattanooga. As it was, the Confederate "siege" of the city had quickly become a farce. By the time the 66th Georgia joined the Army of Tennessee, Bragg's men were the ones under siege. Wretched supply lines kept them on half rations or less, causing hundreds to go over to the Northern army merely to have something to eat.[30] Meanwhile the Federal army opened a new supply line into Chattanooga and received thousands of reinforcements.

It did not take long for Nisbet to join the ranks of Bragg's detractors. "My God!" he recalled. "Where were the glories hard won…? Where were the fruits of victory? *Bragg had frittered away his opportunities by non-action* [emphasis original]." Nearly 40 years after the siege, Nisbet offered several pat solutions to Bragg's problems from the comfort of his Chattanooga study, concluding that the Army of Tennessee "had all the resources [it] needed, except brains."[31]

---

[30] Peter Cozzens, *The Shipwreck of Their Hopes: The Battles for Chattanooga* (Urbana, IL: University of Illinois Press, 1994) 119–20.

[31] Nisbet, *Four Years*, 241–44.

Apart from criticizing Bragg, the young colonel had little to do. He left Hamilton in command of the 66th Georgia, busied himself supervising the placement of brigade pickets, and occasionally dodged sharpshooters' bullets. Nisbet later remembered taking some time off to visit his old stock farm at Cloverdale, even though thousands of Federal soldiers were stationed nearby. Carefully skirting enemy patrols near Lookout Mountain, Nisbet arrived at the farm and found it dilapidated and overgrown. Unable to return the way he came because of roaming Federal cavalry, Nisbet visited old friends in Trenton, dodged another enemy patrol, and returned safely to his lines, along the way supposedly gathering critical data about the movements of the Union army that Bragg ignored.[32]

Three weeks into November, Wilson's Brigade and the rest of Walker's Division were suddenly moved out of Chattanooga Valley. Bragg had become concerned about a possible enemy threat to his right flank, which rested just to the west of Chickamauga Station. Having sent part of the army north to assist another Confederate force near Knoxville, Bragg had stripped that section of his line, at almost the same moment when Union forces began massing across the Tennessee River, directly opposite the critical spot. Alarmed, Bragg quickly recalled his absent units and sent Walker's men to bolster the right.[33]

Wednesday morning, 25 November, found Nisbet's men encamped on the northern end of Missionary Ridge, an 8-mile-long, 500-foot-tall escarpment along which ran most of Bragg's

---

[32] Ibid., 235–41. Nisbet's account of his trip is suspect. It rests on Nisbet's claim that he went to Cloverdale to help some of his slaves there "escape" to the family plantation in Central Georgia, and it features Nisbet "discovering" a great deal of military information that no one in the Confederate army would have known at the time.

[33] Cozzens, *Shipwreck,* 100–105, 116–18, 137–42; Nisbet, *Four Years,* 248–49.

line. The past forty-eight hours had caused some Confederates to doubt that the line could hold. On the 23rd, a massive Federal reconnaissance-in-force had overrun a Confederate outpost at Orchard Knob, just below the ridge. The next day, one heavy enemy column had seized Lookout Mountain, the left anchor of the Army of Tennessee, while another had crossed the Tennessee River, taken position near the Bragg's right, and made ready for an attack.[34]

Bragg could only hope that his right would hold against the assault. Thankfully for him, at that point along Missionary Ridge, on an eminence known as Tunnel Hill because of the railroad that passed through it, there was posted perhaps the best combat unit in his army, a division under General Patrick R. Cleburne. Thankfully, too, the Federal commander facing Cleburne, Major General William T. Sherman, was baffled by the lay of the land and uncertain of Confederate dispositions. Making no use of his vast superiority in numbers and artillery, Sherman attacked piecemeal. By judicious maneuvering, deft use of reserves, and a good bit of luck, Cleburne stymied Sherman.[35]

On Cleburne's left, Nisbet's men spent the day listening to the sounds of battle at Tunnel Hill. They were available to Cleburne if he needed them, but as it turned out he did not. Enforced inactivity did not stop Nisbet from placing himself at Cleburne's shoulder during the entire battle, or so Nisbet claimed in his memoirs. From breaking up an attack with artillery fire, to ordering a timely counterattack, to plugging a gap in Cleburne's lines with the 66th Georgia and 26th Georgia Battalion, Nisbet

---

[34] Cozzens, *Shipwreck,* 15, 128–37, 143–204.

[35] Craig L. Symonds, "Patrick Cleburne's Defense of Tunnel Hill Revisited," *Confederate Generals in the Western Theater, Vol. I: Classic Essays on America's Civil War,* eds., Lawrence Lee Hewitt and Arthur W. Bergeron, Jr. (Knoxville: University of Tennessee Press, 2010) 135–47.

was, in his own mind, the linchpin of Confederate success on Tunnel Hill. In truth, Cleburne had enough artillery at hand, used his own reserves without drawing on Walker's Division, and personally ordered the counterattack.[36] Unless one completely discounts all of the official reports of the action, Nisbet greatly enhanced his role in the battle, assuming that he had any role at all.[37]

After the battle of Tunnel Hill died down, Nisbet told his men to start cooking dinner while he waited further orders. Riding over to a nearby artillery battery, Nisbet encountered General Cleburne, who chastised the colonel for allowing his men to build fires so close to the enemy. When Nisbet protested that his brigade was hungry, Cleburne ordered him to withdraw towards Chickamauga Station and draw rations there. The Army of Tennessee, Cleburne told Nisbet, was leaving Missionary Ridge.[38]

As the 66th Georgia broke camp and marched off, the men slowly became aware of the disaster that had befallen Bragg's army. Shortly after Cleburne's triumph at Tunnel Hill, the Union commander at Chattanooga, General Ulysses S. Grant, ordered the Army of the Cumberland to attack the center of Missionary Ridge, to take some of the pressure off of Sherman. Four divisions of Yankee infantry, 20,000 strong, had captured Confederate rifle

[36] Ibid.; Nisbet, *Four Years*, 249–51. None of the standard works on the Chattanooga Campaign mention Nisbet or the 66th Georgia being sent to Tunnel Hill. Moreover, the 39th Georgia Infantry, which made the counterattack, was part of the brigade of Gen. Alfred Cumming, who was nearby, outranked Nisbet, and therefore was not likely to have taken orders from him.

[37] For an argument implying that Nisbet's men *might* been involved at Tunnel Hill, see "What Were They Doing over There?: Walker's Div. at Chattanooga," TOCWOC—A Civil War Blog, www.brettschulte.net/CWBLOG.

[38] Nisbet, *Four Years*, 252–53.

pits at the base of the ridge, then, with barely a pause, started up the steep slope. Ordinarily, such an attack—uphill, against entrenched, veteran troops—would have been suicidal. Unfortunately for the Confederates, Bragg's line was thin and divided, and it did not enjoy clear fields of fire. Against all odds, the Army of the Cumberland broke right through the Army of Tennessee, capturing thirty cannon and thousands of prisoners. The defeated Confederates withdrew into northern Georgia in great panic.[39] Chattanooga was now firmly in Union hands. Should Grant's forces follow up their victory at Missionary Ridge with a vigorous pursuit, the Army of Tennessee stood in great danger of completely falling apart. Until the Confederates could reach the safety of a stronger position, they needed a rearguard. Nisbet's men were assigned to protect the army's rear.

For the 66th Georgia, still under the command of Lieutenant Colonel Hamilton, the retreat from Missionary Ridge was by turns a harrowing and a comical affair. Ordered to help an artillery battery get away, Hamilton had his men light torches to see their way through the rainy night, located a narrow, overgrown foot path leading back to Chickamauga Station, and set off. The battery got down off Missionary Ridge without any trouble, but then it became stuck in the muddy banks of a creek. "All the profanity and beating of the [horse] drivers could not move them," Nisbet recalled, so the regiment was divided up, one company to each cannon, and waded into the creek to push the battery out. "It is wonderful what eighty-five or ninety-men can accomplish," Nisbet mused, "when 'they put their shoulders to the wheel.'" All of the battery's guns made it to safety.[40]

Nisbet's regiment arrived at Chickamauga Station late that night, long after the Army of Tennessee had passed through and

[39] Cozzens, *Shipwreck,* 244–342.
[40] Nisbet, *Four Years,* 253–54.

set fire to the depot there. Pressed for time, Nisbet broke open the storehouses and allowed his men to take whatever they could carry. After stuffing their haversacks with hardtack and skewering sides of salted meat with their bayonets, the soldiers of the 66th gleefully turned their attention to several barrels of sorghum molasses. Knocking the heads out of the barrels, Nisbet's men scooped up the molasses in their hats. When the syrup levels fell below easy reach, they had to lean over into the barrels. Eventually one man, "a devilish fellow," began to kick his comrades' feet out from under them, plunging them down into the syrup. The other soldiers then fished the sticky victims out of the barrel and scraped the molasses off of them.[41]

Between Chickamauga Station and Dalton, Georgia, the 66th Georgia skirmished with Grant's pursuing columns on 26 November, losing a few of its men. Just as the regiment had missed Chickamauga and Missionary Ridge, however, it was not involved in the closing fight of the Chattanooga Campaign. At Ringgold, 13 miles south of Chickamauga Station, where the Western & Atlantic Railroad cut through a mountain pass, Cleburne's Division took up a strong position until the army's wagon trains could get to safety. While Nisbet's men marched further south, Cleburne stood fast, holding Ringgold against Grant's attacks on 27 November before breaking away. The enemy pursuit was blunted; the Confederate wagon trains and artillery were saved.[42]

Ensconced at Dalton, the Army of Tennessee ended its retreat and counted its losses. Some 6,000 Rebel soldiers had been killed, wounded, or captured in the battles for Chattanooga.[43] Alongside the veterans, Nisbet's rookies had suffered a few casualties. The

[41] Ibid., 255.
[42] Cozzens, *Shipwreck,* 370–84.
[43] Ibid., 389.

regiment had not had any men killed in battle, but five men had been wounded, one of them, Private S. E. Taylor of Company A, badly enough to be permanently disabled. Four men had died of disease during the Chattanooga Campaign; eleven more were sick. Twenty men, including a sergeant and a corporal, had been captured during the retreat, and of these, six would soon die in prisoner-of-war camps. In Company K, Private J. M. Greer had been taken away from the regiment by his mother a week before Missionary Ridge, probably for being under-age and enlisting without permission.[44]

Finally, ten men of the 66th had deserted at Chattanooga. Only three of them left during the retreat. The others had checked out weeks earlier. Either lukewarm Confederates to begin with, or else demoralized by Bragg's inactivity, their own empty bellies, and the growing numbers of Federal troops, the deserters were part of a slow attenuation of Confederate strength that had made it difficult for the Army of Tennessee to hold its positions.

Only four of the ten Chattanooga deserters appear in the census records, making it difficult to draw firm conclusions about them. One deserter was a teenager, another was in his twenties, and the final two were in their forties. The four men hailed from three counties, all far from the front lines, which meant that they could not have been driven to desert by the close proximity of home. Three were poor; the fourth, William Sprayberry, an unpaid volunteer, owned $3,700 in real and personal property as well as a slave.[45] Two of the older deserters were married with children; the younger two were single. No single demographic factor explains why these men left the 66th Georgia.

---

[44] CSRs for S. E. Taylor and J. M. Greer.

[45] William H. Sprayberry CSR; Eighth Census, 1860, Georgia, free inhabitants, Dekalb County; Manuscript Returns of Slaves, Eighth Census, 1860, Georgia, free inhabitants, Dekalb County.

In early December, William Hurst wrote to his wife in Newton County. Hurst had missed the recent excitement because he had been in the rear suffering from a cold. When the army retreated, Hurst temporarily attached himself to another command, where he heard rumors that the 66th had been heavily engaged and lost over half of its strength. Hurst's wife must have heard similar rumors, for he hastened to reassure her: "I recon [sic] you thought I was in [the battle], but I was not…neither was our regiment." Owing to his comrades' inexperience, Hurst added, "I was glad for them that they did not [have to fight]." Hurst bemoaned the loss of precious supplies thrown away on the retreat, his inability to scrounge more than one meal a day, the regiment's ill-sited camp at Dalton, which was "as steep as the roof a house, [making] it bad [for] cooking and sleeping," and the "heavy…gloom" cast over the men by the defeat at Missionary Ridge. "Such times I never saw before," he confessed.[46]

Many soldiers in the Army of Tennessee were just as depressed as Hurst. The Chattanooga Campaign had struck a terrible blow to the army's morale. After Gettysburg, Vicksburg, and Missionary Ridge, many Confederate soldiers considered that they might lose the war, and began to ask themselves: was it worthwhile to fight any longer? Hundreds concluded that it was not, and through the end of the year and beyond, the Army of Tennessee steadily hemorrhaged from desertion. William Campbell, a private in Company E of the 66th Georgia, was among those who gave up after the army had reached Dalton. On the sixth day of December, the thirty-six-year-old hardscrabble farmer snuck out of camp and went back to his family and his 60 acres in Cobb County.[47] Three other soldiers of the 66th did the same later that month. Their

---

[46]Hurst to wife, 3 December 1863, Hurst Papers, KMNBP.

[47]William H. Campbell CSR; Eighth Census, 1860, Georgia, free inhabitants, Cobb County.

absence did not cripple the regiment, but if too many other soldiers followed them, not only the 66th Georgia but the entire Army of Tennessee might simply melt away. Things needed to change, and quickly.

One change that almost immediately boosted spirits in the army was the departure of Braxton Bragg. In fairness to the oft-maligned general, he had been burdened with several fractious and incapable subordinates, forced to defend a weak position, and confronted by a larger number of well-fed and well-led troops. Although some of his generals and a small portion of the rank and file still believed in him, Bragg had probably lost the confidence of most of his men, and he knew it. He was relieved of command at his own request, superseded on 27 December by General Joseph E. Johnston.

The army's new commander came to Dalton under a cloud. Johnston had originally led what became the Army of Northern Virginia, before being badly wounded in 1862 near Richmond and sidelined for almost a year. Johnston's bad luck in getting shot had been preceded by a falling out with President Davis over matters of rank, strategy, and government confidence. The general and the president soon grew to detest each other, and their mutual rancor increased after the fall of Vicksburg, a disaster for which each blamed the other. Davis, lacking other suitable candidates, had appointed Johnston to command the Army of Tennessee only with great reluctance, and Johnston, who believed that Davis was deliberately setting him up for failure, had accepted it with much of the same.[48]

---

[48] Albert Castel, *Decision in the West: The Atlanta Campaign of 1864* (Lawrence: University Press of Kansas, 1992) 29–30; Richard McMurry, *Atlanta 1864: Last Chance for the Confederacy* (Lincoln: University of Nebraska Press, 2000) 10–11.

Whatever Johnston's skills as a strategist, he was capable of repairing the hungry, broken, and disorganized Army of Tennessee. Johnston reversed several unpopular changes that Bragg had made to the army's organization. He curbed disciplinary problems by reinstituting regular guard duty and drill, which kept the men occupied and out of trouble. He got supplies flowing to Dalton by threatening to retreat if they were not forthcoming. He ensured that fresh, slaughtered beef was delivered to the camps every day; he staged mock battles to hone the combat instincts of his men; and he regularly dispensed tobacco and whiskey rations. Johnston's men appreciated all of his efforts, and they began to delight in their new commander. Two months after the change in command, Private Charles Davis of Company K boasted, "The men are all in good spirits, & have Great confidence in old Joe."[49]

Though it was a relatively fresh unit, the 66th Georgia benefited from the new state of affairs. Many in the regiment had left Macon and Atlanta without receiving necessary items. Others had lost personal and company baggage during the retreat from Chattanooga. Company requisition forms show the extent of need in the regiment. During the last week of December, 1863, Nisbet's officers requested 326 shirts, 292 pairs of underdrawers, 231 pairs of pants, 163 rugs (often used as blankets slung over the shoulder in a roll while on the march), 138 jackets, 58 pairs of

---

[49]Castel, *Decision in the West*, 33–34; Andrew Haughton, *Training, Tactics and Leadership in the Confederate Army of Tennessee: Seeds of Failure* (London: Frank Cass Publishers, 2000) 139–41, 144–47; Larry J. Daniel, *Soldiering in the Army of Tennessee* (Chapel Hill: University of North Carolina Press, 1991) 26, 32, 59, 60–63, 103, 139; Charles W. Davis to Prior L. Davis, 25 February 1864, cited in *Teaching American History: The Quest for Relevancy,* ed. Allan O. Kownslar (National Council for the Social Studies, 1974) 54.

shoes, 25 woolen blankets, 21 water buckets and mess pans, 13 camp kettles, 10 axes, 9 picks, 3 coffins, and 1 officer's tent.[50]

Thanks to Johnston's efforts, most of these requisitions were filled. The following February, only shirts (84), pants (57 pairs), socks (51 pairs), and shoes (43 pairs) seemed lacking. However, Confederate shortages and the needs of other armies kept Johnston from solving all of the supply problems. In March, 1864, requisitions spiked again, with Nisbet's officers asking for 135 jackets, 89 pairs of pants, 69 pairs of shoes, 48 pairs of socks, 39 pairs of drawers, 10 mess pans, 6 water buckets and 4 camp kettles, as well as 6 1/2 bunches of braid for officers' uniforms. All things considered, the regiment got most of what it needed. Nisbet even got a shirt, jacket and pair of pants for himself.[51]

New uniforms and camp items and more regular rations were part of what kept the Army of Tennessee together at Dalton. The other elements were a sense of shared hardship, religious revivals, and deterrent punishments. Unlike Lee's soldiers, "the Army of Tennessee lacked battlefield victories" that might have provided a source of solidarity; rather, "its unity was grass roots in nature." Believing that shared misery was a lighter burden, that God would protect them, or that the long arm of military justice would deal with them, Johnston's men found the strength to pull together.[52]

The men of the 66th Georgia certainly complained that winter about hard times. "I am all alone...blessed with a terrible fit of the blues," Lieutenant Briggs Napier confessed to his girlfriend, Bessie. "Since...Macon it seems...the time has been one of toil &

---

[50] CSRs for Josiah Adams, Lorenzo Belisle, Moses Brown, A. H. Coates, James Hendon, Charles Holmes, Ellis Hull, Thomas Kernaghan, Thomas Langston, Henry Parks, A. C. Patman, Isaac Reese, William R. Ross, John Rosser, John F. Smith, Osborne Stone, A. J. Summers, John Terrell, A. H. C. Walker, William Weaver, and J. A. Wright.

[51] Ibid. Unfiled item, Nisbet CSR.

[52] Daniel, *Soldiering*, 21–23.

exposure." Sergeant Crane had "a very poor Christmas," enlivened only by some eggnog concocted by Lieutenant James Hendon. William Hurst likened his service to "bondage...enough to dishartin anybody." Mindful of disheartening his kin, Hurst clung to his Camp Cobb mantra—"I believe I am about as cheerful as almost anyone"—even though he did not seem to believe it.[53]

Letters from the soldiers of the 66th during this period expressed desires to go home, or at least to escape fighting. Hurst was overjoyed when his wife told him she had found a substitute, "for I assure you I am very tired of the camp life and want to get home, probably as bad you all could wish me home." John Morgan Davis, a sergeant in Company G, was by turns anxious to get a non-combat assignment, a leave of absence, or a substitute: "You may tell [John Woods] he can have me...if he will detail me out of the army[,] at almost any price he wants...I will esteem it...a great favor to be relieved from this place"; then, "Mary if you know of anyone that will join this Company and send him to me I can get a forty days furlow [sic]"; finally, "I am sorry Spinks would not come as a Recruit for me...I have give up all hope of getting out." Lieutenant Ross feared that only a wound would bring him home again, "& fighting is an ingredient which was left out of my Composition, so I see no chance from that source." The only soldier who seemed to prefer the company of the army to that of family was Private William T. Farrar. "I don't think I could stay at home long if I was there," Farrar told a lady friend,

---

[53] Briggs H. Napier to Bessie Reed, 3 April 1864, Briggs H. Napier Family Collection, Middle Georgia Archives; James P. Crane to sister, 29 December 1863, Crane letters, AHC; Hurst to wife, 24 December 1863, Hurst papers, MNBP.

"before I could get lonesome & tired and would want to get back hear [sic]."[54]

Hurst, Sergeant Davis, and Ross expressed no particular loyalty to their regiment.[55] Taken literally, their words suggest that, when faced with hardships, they would rather abandon the Confederate cause than suffer for it. In the end, all three stuck it out at Dalton. Did they have or develop an unspoken sense of pride in the 66th Georgia during the winter? Did personal honor demand that they stay and fight? The latter seems more likely, at least in the case of Sergeant Davis. "Pray that I may return to you *in Honor as becomes a Soldier*," Davis urged his wife. "Pray that I may never dishonor the name of Soldier" (emphasis added).[56]

What also increased solidarity in the ranks was the growing sense that there was no one else to turn to, even at home. True, married soldiers could confide in their wives, and younger soldiers might lean on their families. To some observant soldiers, though, the Southern people as a whole seemed complacent and half-hearted by 1864, no longer willing to sacrifice for the common good.

R. J. Delph, a South Carolina-born soldier in the 66th, put his finger on the pulse of Confederate home front morale and felt it fading. "In the commencement of our difficulties," Delph told his hometown newspaper, "our people *at home* were enthusiastic, energetic and patriotic… Our soldiers felt that *soldiers* were honored and respected, [and] the Ladies greeted their every step to

---

[54] Hurst to wife, 31 December 1863, Hurst papers; John M. Davis to wife, 29 December 1863, and two undated letters, Civil War Miscellany, GDAH; Ross to sister, 3 March 1864, BNRR Collection; William T. Farrar to Eliza Rains, 1 March 1864, Civil War Miscellany, GDAH.

[55] Many later-enlisting Confederate soldiers felt the same way: "Unit [i.e., regimental] pride proved much less important than primary group [i.e., company or mess] solidarity" (Noe, *Reluctant Rebels,* 156–62).

[56] Davis to wife, 29 December 1863, Civil War Miscellany, GDAH.

and from the Army." Three years of war had changed all that; "Our people have degenerated, and have lost sight of the object that stimulated our rulers to throw off the accursed yoke [of] Yankee rule." Sensing this diminished spirit in letters from home, Confederate soldiers began to ask themselves, "What are we here for? Why have we sacrificed the comforts of home, family, 'and the pursuit of happiness'?"[57]

Greed, Delph declared, was responsible for this evil state of affairs. Soldiers' families were paying "exorbitant—aye, *extortionate* prices…for necessaries" from their neighbors, who, "when they will part with their supplies." Of cordwood, corn, flour, potatoes, and butter, charged five, twenty, or sometimes sixty times the prewar values. At the front, with little money himself—and much of it inflated and worthless—the average Confederate private could do nothing except take the "long and almost unconscious walk" of desertion.[58]

Corruption, self-seeking, and willful blindness towards the needs of their neighbors now characterized the Southern people. "We believe," Delph concluded, "that we have enemies at home that are far-far-worse than the Yankees… A large majority of our people…being confined respectively to their different limits, have no interest in our welfare." Where "once [we] thought to be a soldier was to be honored," the young private and his fellows had begun to "feel degraded, because of [our] treatment [by] the people at home, who should be our friends."[59]

Surviving letters from Southern civilians to Confederate soldiers are quite uncommon, so it is hard to say whether those who supported the 66th Georgia were becoming demoralized. The few known letters from soldiers' wives convey little loss of faith.

---

[57] *Edgefield Advertiser,* 3 February 1864.
[58] Ibid.
[59] Ibid.

Neither John Davis's wife nor William Hurst's wife suggested desertion to their husbands, though both worried about managing worn-down farms, boisterous children, and stubborn slaves by themselves. Mostly, they urged their men to keep their heads down, stay safe, trust in God and do their duty.[60]

One letter to a soldier in the 66th mentioned demoralized neighbors, but avowed intense personal devotion to the Confederate cause. Writing to her husband, J. D. Bowdoin of Company B, an Adairsville woman grieved that since Federal troops had occupied the town, "skores of our best Secess [sic] are [swearing allegiance to the] union...here...Oh what a set of cowardly thieves we have to contend with here." Not for her any craven submission; she had always been Confederate, and "if I had been union I should desolve the union with the devils now shure." The certainty that Union and Confederate forces would battle again excited the woman, even though she could not participate, for "I can now hear the cannon and feel ready to exclaim Glory. Why I am not able to tell but it raises my spirits and makes me feel better."[61] Allowing that some of her feistiness was meant to inspire her husband, it still stands to reason that the sentiments were honest.

Some Confederates hoped that pious, charitable religion would lighten heavy hearts on the home front and erase the sins causing Confederate defeats. Cleansing a society, however, would do little good unless Confederate regiments received a dose of the same medicine. Religious revivals swept through the armies in winter 1863 and may have given the Confederate cause at least another

---

[60] Mary Davis to John M. Davis, undated (but contents suggest February) 1864, Civil War Miscellany, GDAH; Mary B. Hurst to William Hurst, 29 December 1863 and 1 May 1864, Hurst Papers, KMNBP.

[61] Unknown to J. D. Bowdoin, 23 June 1864, Regimental Files, Georgia, KMNBP.

year of life by keeping men in the ranks. Tens of thousands reportedly became new Christians or recommitted their lives to God. Confederate soldiers' confidence in divine favor, divine protection, and divine justice, coupled with security in the hereafter, helped many of them to face death and defeat without murmuring or faltering.[62]

In the 66th Georgia, William Hurst waxed most spiritual. "Our trials are great," Hurst admitted in the aftermath of Missionary Ridge, "but the Lord is able to deliver us out of them." On Christmas Eve, Hurst proclaimed that "the Lord only knows how long this scurge [sic] is to be upon us." He urged his family to "be reconciled to all of God's providential dealings with us, knowing that what he does is rite [sic] and will work for our good if…we are his true followers." Hurst praised his wife for a spiritually consoling letter in early April: "I do hope your prayers may be answered on our behalf…but if it be otherwise ordered let us not murmer [sic] but [submit] to the will of our heavenly Father." Towards the end of the month, Hurst made a rare complaint about army morals: "The pore soldier has the imperfections of human nature to contend with in camps as well as at home"—and declared that "if any of the human race is saved, it will be by grace and grace alone." Overall, Hurst's tone that winter was one of hope.[63]

Hurst came into the Confederate Army with a firm religious background, as evinced by his earliest letters from Camp Cobb. None of the other sparse writings from the regiment displayed the same depth of religious feeling. Sergeant Davis placed himself in the hands of God—"to him alone I look for help,"—but his wife was uncertain of his salvation; "I do hope you are one of the

---

[62] Ibid.; Wiley, *Life of Johnny Reb*, 171–91.
[63]Hurst to wife, 3 and 24 December 1863 and 2 and 18 April 1864, Hurst letters, KMNBP.

Lord's people," she replied. Sergeant Crane appreciated a bible and a Sunday school book given by the Ladies Volunteer Association of Augusta, and applauded on some preaching he heard at Dalton, but shared nothing about his own faith. Nor did these chroniclers plumb the effects of the revivals on the regiment.[64] It could be that most, like Hurst, were already Christians when they joined the Confederate Army. It could be, too, that Nisbet's men were similar to other late-war Confederate soldiers, preferring a home-based Christianity tying soldier to family, rather than a camp-based faith tying soldier to fellow soldier. Though many were pious, "a majority of [later-enlisting men] never wrote about religion." Thus, the absence of spiritual talk amongst most of Nisbet's men might not be unusual.[65]

Punishments evoked even less commentary than religious matters. Only Sergeant Davis spoke of them. "We are compelled to witness another painful sight yesterday," Davis wrote the day after New Year's. "A man belonging to this regiment was shot for deserting." The convicted man's division was drawn up in an open square, with the prisoner on the open side, sitting on his coffin. A twelve-man firing party was given a mixture of loaded and unloaded guns, so that none would know who had fired the fatal shot. After the execution, the division was then marched slowly by the coffin, to see their comrade's riddled body and reflect on his fate. Sergeant Davis got the message: "I hope never to see another such sight."[66] Though neither Nisbet nor any of the other men in the regiment mentioned any serious disciplinary problems at

---

[64]John M. Davis to Mary Davis, undated (but contents suggest February) 1864, and Mary Davis to John M. Davis, undated (but again contents suggest February), Civil War Miscellany, GDAH; Crane to sister, 29 December 1863, Crane to father, 17 April 1864, Crane letters, AHC.

[65] Noe, *Reluctant Rebels,* 132–33, 138, 143, 150.

[66] John N. Davis to wife, 2 January 1864, cited in Daniel, *Soldiering,* 112.

Dalton, the execution showed that the 66th Georgia had at least a few troublemakers in its ranks.

Apart from the unnamed, executed man, eighteen soldiers in Nisbet's regiment deserted during late 1863. It cannot be determined whether they left before reaching Chattanooga, after retreating to Dalton, or in the last few days of the year. Only one of the eighteen can be found in the census records: John Mitchell, the eighteen-year-old son of a poor Gordon County farmer. Gordon is in upstate Georgia, so Mitchell might have left simply because he was close to home.[67]

Mitchell had plenty of company that winter. At least 1,365 Georgia soldiers left the ranks between December 1863 and 30 April 1864, and took an oath of allegiance to the Union. Some came from Lee's Army of Northern Virginia, but the vast majority came from Johnston's command. Despite his reputation for leniency, Johnston offered little of it to recaptured deserters. It has even been argued that Johnston shot as many men during the first two months of 1864 as the notoriously strict Bragg did during his entire tenure.[68]

From October or November 1863 until January 1864, Nisbet was in command of Wilson's Georgia Brigade, by virtue of Wilson's untimely death and his own position as ranking colonel. On 20 January, Nisbet turned the brigade over to Brigadier General Clement H. Stevens. Born in Connecticut but raised in South Carolina, the forty-seven-year-old Stevens had led the 24th

---

[67] John C. Mitchell CSR; Seventh Census, 1850, Georgia, free inhabitants, Gordon County.

[68] Mark Alan Weitz, "A Higher Duty: Desertion among Georgia Troops during the Civil War" (PhD Diss., Arizona State University, 1998) 117–21; Haughton, *Training, Tactics and Leadership*, 141–42.

South Carolina Infantry at Chickamauga, where he had been wounded.[69]

Nisbet took an immediate liking to Stevens. "He was a man…of splendid physique," Nisbet later mused, "well versed in military education and experience…and although a strict disciplinarian, he soon gained the confidence and esteem of his officers and men." A few of Nisbet's officers emphasized Stevens's exacting discipline in their letters, and not kindly. Adjutant William LeConte resented the general for torpedoing a winter furlough. "If [General Stevens] had made the application when I wished I would be home now," LeConte informed his mother, "but he is quite obstinate and would not agree with me." Lieutenant Ross also locked horns with Stevens, over some unnamed offence. "I thought he was going to put me under arrest," Ross wrote, "but he let me off by saying don't do so anymore which I don't think I will." Stevens's men took to calling him "Old Rock," which Nisbet thought a compliment, although Ross thought it referenced Stevens's unbending nature: "He is a hard case too."[70]

For his part, Stevens thought that Nisbet's men were substandard soldiers. He complained that of all the units in his "very small…inferior" brigade, the 66th Georgia and 26th Georgia Battalion were the worst. Stevens described both as "chiefly [drawn] from exempt and discharged soldiers…such inferior physical material that they will melt away before the end of one week's march." Nisbet's men, Stevens decided, should have remained on garrison duty in Florida; "for such duty I think they will answer, for [combat duty] they will not." Stevens sought to

---

[69] Warner, *Generals in Gray*, 291–92.
[70] Nisbet, *Four Years*, 263; William LeConte to mother, 28 February 1864, Civil War Miscellany, GDAH; Ross to mother, 3 March 1864, BNRR Collection.

get rid of the 66th Georgia, even if he did not receive another regiment as replacement.[71]

Though Stevens did not get his wish, he might have been pleased that that the regiment's officer corps was shaken up. At General Johnston's order, examination boards were established to review the qualifications of regimental officers and remove those found wanting. In the 66th Georgia, the boards pruned away four lieutenants and one captain. For each of the lieutenants—Thomas Atkinson, Benjamin Hammock, John McDade, and Wiley Quillian—"limited education" was the rationale for dismissal. Well-meaning, they were nonetheless unqualified to lead. It was suggested that they be accepted into other regiments, but as far as the records show, none of the four went back into service.[72]

There was less sympathy or understanding for Captain Jesse Thornton of Company I. Whether Thornton had forgotten the lessons of military service in Ramsey's 1st Georgia, or never learned them at all, Nisbet had lost all patience with him by April 1864. Writing to Secretary of War Seddon, Nisbet catalogued Thornton's flaws: "[He] is inefficient…[and] His morals are such as to render him a bad disciplinarian." Nisbet recounted how Thornton had recently been court-martialed for disobeying orders and displaying "a mutinous conduct," and recommended that he be dropped from the army rolls.[73]

Thornton tried to salve his humiliation by admitting that he was "incompetent physically to serve in the infantry," and asked to join another branch of service. Nisbet allowed that Thornton might do well as a cavalryman, but dismissed Thornton's

---

[71] Clement H. Stevens to unnamed, 10 April 1864, South Caroliniana Collection, University of South Carolina.

[72] CSRs for Thomas J. P. Atkinson, Benjamin F. Hammock, J. H. McDade, and Wiley H. Quillian.

[73] Nisbet to James P. Seddon, 7 April 1864, Thornton CSR.

mitigating claims of disability. The captain's real problem, according to Nisbet, was his bad character. Kicked out of the company that he had raised, Thornton became a private in the 5th Georgia Infantry, another regiment in the Army of Tennessee.[74]

Inefficiency was not the only cause of officer attrition. Several weak constitutions had broken under physical stress. Captain Alexander Reid of Company F still suffered from his early-war abdominal wound, and in January 1864 he took a long leave of absence because of it. At home, his condition worsened, leaving Reid with a "turmid abdomen, dry skin, debility," and a constant discharge of "fecal matters." Believing himself disabled, Reid resigned on 11 March. Lieutenant J. A. Wright of Company B followed Reid in early April, citing poor health and the desire to join the cavalry.[75] By the time the snow had melted around Dalton, the 66th Georgia had lost almost one-third of its original officers corps.

The common soldiers of the 66th were not privy to the examination boards or the private displeasures of General Stevens. They were, however, told in late February to be ready to move at a moment's notice. Could there be a battle up ahead, some of Nisbet's men wondered, as they marched north out of Dalton and took position, halfway between their camp and Tunnel Hill? Sergeant Davis thought so. "There is heavy cannonading all day," he wrote his wife. "We think the Time not fare [sic] distant that a great effort will be made to crush us." In reserve, the men of the 66th Georgia remained ignorant of the situation.[76]

---

[74] Thornton to Seddon, 22 April 1864 (Nisbet's endorsement, 23 April), Thornton CSR.

[75] Alexander H. Reid to Samuel Cooper, 11 March 1864, Reid CSR; J. A. Wright to Cooper, 1 April 1864, Wright CSR.

[76] Davis to wife, undated (but contents suggest February) 1864, Civil War Miscellany, GDAH.

What had happened was a multi-pronged Federal raid, launched to destroy the Confederacy's infrastructure. Yankee columns in Mississippi got busy wrecking Southern railroads in the eastern part of the state. To keep Johnston from thwarting the raid, part of the Federal forces in Chattanooga advanced on Dalton and occupied Johnston's attention. After some desultory skirmishing, the Federals had withdrawn, leaving behind twisted railroad metal.[77]

The 66th Georgia never came within a rifled musket shot of the skirmish, but that did not preclude a bit of boasting about the victory. The Yankees had been "whipt [sic] handily and driven...back fifteen or twenty miles," according to Private William Farrar, or "whipped...so bad they incontinently skedaddled back toward Chattanooga," in the words of Adjutant LeConte.[78] After almost a year without a real fight, perhaps these two and many others in the regiment enjoyed experiencing battle vicariously.

Drill, guard duty, building shelters, begging family for care packages, waiting in reserve near a battle—this was how the men of the 66th Georgia spent their first winter in the Confederate Army. On 22 March, there was a pleasant diversion from routine when five inches of snow fell on Dalton. Individual "snow ball battles" gave way to a mass engagement pitting Cheatham's Tennessee division against Walker's Georgians. Nisbet and his regiment were chased out of their camps, and when Nisbet led a counorcharge, the Tennesseans pulled him off his horse and carried him away as a "prisoner." The colonel did not blame his men for the icy rout, for they were inexperienced at this type of warfare. "It was the first snow-ball [battle]....my regiment ever

---

[77] Castel, *Decision in the West*, 43–54.
[78] Farrar to Eliza Raines, 1 March 1864, and LeConte to family, 28 February 1864, Civil War Miscellany, GDAH.

saw," Nisbet explained, "consequently they did not understand making ammunition with deftness and celerity."[79]

Would the 66th Georgia perform better on a real battlefield? They would soon find out. Late in April orders came from Johnston to send all non-essential baggage to the rear, a sure sign that the campaign season was about to begin.[80] Three letters written in the late winter and early spring by members of the 66th Georgia must have voiced the sentiments of many others. The first, from Private Delph to curious South Carolinians: "The general feeling and sentiment of this army has changed wonderfully since I last wrote you. Confidence seems to have dethroned despondency, and all are cheerful; determination seems to be depicted in every countenance, which makes one hopeful..."[81] The second, from Private Farrar to his friend: "We have a good many Yanks to contend with up hear but I hope that we will come out successful and whip them out... I think we will fight them harder than we ever did before[;] we aught to..."[82] The third, from Sergeant Davis to his wife: A few more efforts will decide our fait [sic] either Victory or death... If I fall in battle I fall in defence of my country my rights my Family... We do not know how soon our country will be overrun and you may have to move from the enemy don't be alarmed at this but wach [sic]..."[83] If Delph was right, and if the Army of Tennessee was lucky, Farrar might have what he wished, and Davis might be spared a sacrifice; only time would tell.

---

[79] Nisbet, *Four Years*, 269.

[80] Castel, *Decision in the West*, 119.

[81] *Edgefield Advertiser*, 13 April 1864.

[82] Farrar to Raines, 1 March 1864, Civil War Miscellany, GDAH.

[83] Davis to wife, undated (but contents suggest February) 1864, Civil War Miscellany, GDAH.

Chapter 5

"The Regiment Give Out":
The Atlanta Campaign

"Well, Nisbet; what would our leader, Stonewall, think of us?" Lieutenant Colonel Hamilton asked his superior on 1 May 1864, near the tiny North Georgia town of Resaca. "Going eighteen miles to the rear to guard a bridge; at the beginning of a campaign?"[1] Resaca, located 12 miles south of Dalton, was the site of a depot for the Western & Atlantic Railroad. At Resaca, the railroad crossed the Oostanaula River on its way to Atlanta. By seizing Resaca, an enemy force might cut off the Army of Tennessee from its lines of supply and communication. Such an important site needed protection, so the 66th Georgia and the 26th Georgia Battalion had been detached from Walker's Division to guard it.[2]

Nisbet probably preferred to be at Dalton; there, he could take part in a great battle. When Major General William T. Sherman, the new Union commander at Chattanooga, brought his massive three-army force into Georgia, he would surely attack Dalton, where the Confederates had fortified strong natural positions. If the Army of Tennessee could beat back Sherman's attack, then perhaps Johnston could go on the offensive and recapture Chattanooga.

---

[1] James C. Nisbet, *Four Years on the Firing Line* (Chattanooga TN: Imperial Press, 1911) 270.

[2] Ibid.; Castel, *Decision in the West,* 138.

The hopes of many Southerners were riding on the possible successes of Johnston and his men. Indeed, Confederate newspaper editors, politicians, soldiers, and civilians all expected 1864 to be the decisive year of the war. In spite of heavy losses and shrinking borders, the Confederacy remained formidable. The capital, Richmond, was still in Confederate hands, and industrial centers like Atlanta continued to produce weapons, ammunition, and accoutrements. More importantly, the Confederacy fielded two large and potent armies, the Army of Northern Virginia and the Army of Tennessee. All that the Confederacy had to do in 1864, according to its leaders, was hold onto what it had, inflict as many casualties as possible, and avoid losing a big battle or a key city until November. Then, the war-weary Northern people, who would be going to the polls, would have to admit that they could never conquer the South. Lincoln would be cast out; a new, peacemaking president would take office; and the Confederacy would have its independence. Johnston's part of this strategy was to stop Sherman's armies in Northern Georgia, keeping them away from the state's mills and factories, its rich farmlands, and Atlanta.

For the first seven days of May, all Southern reports had Sherman dancing to Johnston's tune. Almost 100,000 Yankees converged on Dalton from the north and northwest. Safe atop the steep slopes of Rocky Face Ridge, Johnston's men fended off Sherman on 7 and 8 May. Meanwhile, at Resaca, Nisbet listened to the sound of the distant cannons.

Then, on the evening of the 8th, Nisbet learned that someone wanted to see him. A slave girl who lived nearby told the colonel that she had been on an errand to Resaca to buy medicine for her ailing mistress. As she had passed through Snake Creek Gap—a long, narrow defile just west of the town—on the way home, several blue-coated soldiers had stopped the girl and taken her horse. She had escaped, but not before catching sight of another group of horsemen heading towards Resaca. "I think [they] are Yankees," she told Nisbet. Nisbet informed Johnston that Sherman's cavalry was in Snake Creek Gap, and Johnston sent some of his own cavalry to explore. After a short, sharp fight, the Confederate cavalry withdrew, and Nisbet was given some alarming news: more than 20,000 of Sherman's infantry under General James B. McPherson had control of the gap.[3]

"I was very uneasy that night," Nisbet later recalled, "for I realized that McPherson could capture Resaca if he advanced in force." Nisbet felt better when two fresh Confederate regiments arrived at Resaca on the 9th, accompanied by a ranking officer, Brigadier General James Cantey, who took responsibility for defending the town. Nisbet's relief turned to concern when the inexperienced Cantey disregarded Nisbet's suggestion to post the entire force inside a small, earthen fort near the railroad bridge. Instead, Cantey sent his own regiments onto an open ridge west of Resaca, and left Nisbet's men in the fort.[4]

When McPherson's Federals emerged from Snake Creek Gap later that morning, they routed Cantey's badly outnumbered men. Nisbet and some of the officers of the 66th had to rally the fleeing Confederates, a job which Nisbet thought Cantey should be doing himself. Searching for Cantey, Nisbet found the general huddled in a bomb-proof shelter inside the fort. "I am ready to receive your orders," Nisbet said with disdain. "Well," Cantey replied, "I want you to take your Regiment and Battalion, and drive the enemy from that ridge." Nisbet did not think that his men stood a chance in the open, but determined to "show them there's somebody here that can fight."[5]

---

[3] Nisbet, *Four Years,* 270–71.
[4] Ibid., 272–73.
[5] Ibid., 273–74.

Joining his regiment, Nisbet explained the plan. They would not try to recapture the ridge, as Cantey had ordered. Instead, they would move into a ravine along Camp Creek, below the ridge. There they would wait until the advancing Federal soldiers reached the near slope. Silhouetted against the sky, the Yankees would make perfect targets. In this manner, Nisbet's men might put up enough resistance to hold Resaca.[6]

At a signal, the 66th Georgia scurried into the ravine without being seen, and the men trained their muskets on the ridgeline. Every time McPherson's men came within range, Nisbet's men mowed them down and drove them back. The plan was working well, but Nisbet realized that eventually the Federals would extend their lines beyond his and surround him. After begging General Cantey in vain for reinforcements, Nisbet reluctantly withdrew. McPherson's soldiers fired on Nisbet's men as they scrambled out of the ravine, and killed or wounded several before the Georgians reached the bridge fort.[7] Nevertheless, Nisbet claimed that his bold defense bluffed McPherson into complete timidity. Though Sherman had ordered McPherson to destroy the railroad, McPherson did not do so, and before the sun had set, McPherson's men were falling back the way they had come. Finally alerted to the danger on his left, Johnston withdrew in saftey from Dalton to Resaca.[8]

Such is Nisbet's account of what he might have considered his finest hour in the Atlanta Campaign. It should be treated with caution. Nisbet and his men were at Resaca, they helped defend the town against McPherson, and McPherson did not take Resaca on 9 May. Apart from these facts, a comparison with other sources points up some embellishments on the part of Nisbet.

[6] Ibid. 274.
[7] Ibid., 274–75.
[8] Ibid., 275–77.

What did General Johnston know about the situation at Resaca? Absolutely nothing, according to Nisbet. Johnston, the colonel wrote, had no idea of McPherson's location until the Yankees appeared in Snake Creek Gap. This is only partly true. Johnston's cavalry had been tracking McPherson for several days, but Johnston believed that McPherson's real target was Rome.[9]

Nisbet certainly claimed credit for sounding the alert at Resaca, a claim that rested on the absence of General Cantey. *"Cantey did not reach Resaca till the morning of the 9th of May,"* Nisbet wrote, and though "he should have made a report of [what happened], he did not," because *"He had good reasons for keeping quiet"* (emphases original). Nisbet's snide commentary aside, the *Official Records* show that Cantey *was* at Resaca when the Confederates discovered McPherson, and that it was he who reported the presence of Federals in Snake Creek Gap.[10]

Nisbet might be forgiven for magnifying his performance at Resaca, particularly as it was the first time he had directed the 66th in combat. No other sources from Nisbet's men mention the stand in the Camp Creek ravine.[11] Federal officers at Snake Creek Gap admired the "rapid musketry" of the Confederates, but reported that it had little effect. Furthermore, the 66th Georgia

---

[9] Castel, *Decision in the West*, 127–30, 136.

[10] Nisbet, *Four Years*, 276, 278; US War Department, *The War of the Rebellion: A Compilation of the Official Records of the Union and Confederate Armies* (Washington, DC: US Government Printing Office, 1880–1901) vol. 38, pt. 4, p. 678 (Hereafter cited as *OR*; all citations are from series 1 unless otherwise noted.).

[11] LeConte wrote about one of the regiment's sharpshooters killing a Yankee sniper at Resaca, but this event took place near a "river" (the Oostanaula?), not the ridge and ravine where Nisbet claimed to have fought. The incident referred to might have taken place during the Battle of Resaca (14–15 May 1864) or sometime later in the campaign ("Events of My Life," 21).

lost a mere three men killed and two wounded at Resaca.[12] Is this proof of a cost-effective defense against overwhelming odds, or a suggestion that the fighting was not as sustained as Nisbet remembered it?

One final detail should be mentioned. The most thorough history of the Atlanta Campaign notes that the Confederate cavalry that reconnoitered Snake Creek Gap had been told to watch for fellow soldiers guarding it.[13] As Nisbet recalled, the only Confederate troops at Resaca that evening were his. This raises two possibilities: either Nisbet learned about McPherson's approach from his own pickets (which should make us wonder why he credited the discovery to a slave girl) or else Nisbet disregarded an order to post guards in Snake Creek Gap. If the latter scenario is plausible, then Nisbet might have been partly responsible for the near disaster at Resaca. Perhaps Nisbet cast himself as a brave, sagacious and level-headed commander on 9 May in order to cover up his own embarrassment.

Whatever the truth of Nisbet's account, the withdrawal of McPherson allowed the Army of Tennessee to reach Resaca and hold off Sherman in two days of battle (14–15 May 1864). Johnston had escaped Sherman's trap, but he had also been forced to abandon Dalton. This set a pattern for the rest of the campaign:

---

[12] *OR,* vol. 38, pt. 3, p. 376. One of the regiment's casualties was Capt. Columbus Jordan, Company B (Columbus M. Jordan compiled service record (CSR), National Archives and Records Administration [NARA], Washington, DC [All CSR citations are for the 66th Georgia Infantry unless otherwise noted.]). Nisbet wrote that Jordan was wounded in the leg during the withdrawal to the fort and died of infection several days later. Jordan's CSR dates his wound to 18 May 1864 at "Resaca," but the Army of Tennessee had left Resaca two days earlier. Assuming that Nisbet is correct about Jordan dying as a result of combat, there may have been an error in transcription (Nisbet, *Four Years,* 275).

[13] Castel, *Decision in the West,* 137.

Johnston would choose a formidable position, dig in, and wait for Sherman to attack; Sherman would hold Johnston's attention in front while sending part of his force to get around Johnston's flank; and Johnston would then be forced to fight at a disadvantage or retreat. In each case, Johnston chose to pull back. Within a month, Sherman pushed Johnston 60 miles closer to Atlanta.

On a few occasions, the pattern temporarily changed. At Cassville, 28 miles south of Resaca, Johnston took a stand on 19 May and tried to ambush Sherman. Nisbet, his men, and the rest of the Army of Tennessee cheered at Johnston's announcement that there would be no more falling back and that Johnston himself would lead them into battle. "Our army was ready," Nisbet remembered, "in good spirits, and anxious to meet the enemy." Unfortunately for Johnston, wayward Federal cavalry blundered into his flank and panicked some of his subordinates, forcing Johnston to scrap his plans. Nisbet blamed Lieutenant General John Bell Hood, one of Johnston's corps commanders, for failing to spring the trap and for convincing Johnston to retreat again.[14] A week after Cassville, Johnston fought Sherman to a standstill near Dallas. Two Federal defeats there, at New Hope Church (25 May 1864) and Pickett's Mill (27 May 1864), cost Sherman 3,000 casualties. One month later, an impatient Sherman, bogged down by muddy roads, tried to break through Johnston's line with a frontal assault at Kennesaw Mountain (27 June 1864). Another 3,000 Yankees fell, against Confederate losses of about 700.

Johnston's victories near Dallas and at Kennesaw Mountain boosted his army's spirits, but they did not halt Sherman. After regrouping, resupplying, and waiting for better weather, Sherman

---

[14] Castel, *Decision in the West*, 200; Nisbet, *Four Years*, 290.

again threatened Johnston's flank and compelled the Confederates to retreat. Even after receiving reinforcement in mid-May, Johnston still fought defensively, retreating whenever pressed. With each retreat, more Georgia territory was lost, and Jefferson Davis grew more concerned. Beginning in late June, Davis began to consider replacing Johnston with a bolder commander.[15]

Because both Sherman and Johnston were tactically cautious, there were few pitched battles in Northern Georgia, and so Nisbet's men experienced little sustained combat. Instead there were almost daily skirmishes, and these drew blood. In a picket clash in mid-June, Sergeant Isham J. Davis of Company K saw his brother, Charles, a private in the same company, shot in the neck. Isham rushed to Charles's side, but Charles died in seconds, without uttering a word. With Nisbet's permission, Isham went to the rear bearing his brother's body. "We dug the grave 2½ feet deep," Isham told his planter father, Prior, "and roped him in a blanket and lay him in the grave."[16] Preceding Charles in death were two men killed near Dallas; the following week, eight more soldiers in Nisbet's regiment were wounded at Kennesaw. Seventeen were captured between May and early July.[17]

Nisbet's men avenged their losses with a sortie against the Federal trenches near Kennesaw Mountain. After the Federal assault on 27 June had failed, the Yankees had crept ever closer to Johnston's line, intending to lay siege. To forestall this, Johnston's generals to launched a few raids. In Walker's Division, several

---

[15] Castel, *Decision in the West,* 208–10; McMurry, *Last Chance for the Confederacy,* 46–47, 88.

[16] Isham J. Davis to Prior L. Davis, 26 June 1864, Davis family papers, private collection.

[17] A 10 June 1864 issue of the *Atlanta Southern Confederacy* listed seventeen casualties in the regiment over an unknown period. One month later, the *Macon Daily Telegraph* named sixty-six men who been killed, wounded, or gone missing "since the campaign opened" (19 July 1864).

hundred volunteers, perhaps including some men of the 66th Georgia, organized raiding parties armed with .44 caliber, seven-shot Colt revolvers. On a selected night, the raiders set out in the darkness, attacked the Federal picket line, and captured many Yankee soldiers. The raiders returned to their lines, prisoners in tow, just as the stunned Federals opened fire with artillery.[18]

Germs and viruses proved more deadly to Nisbet's men than bullets and shells. Various illnesses killed at least twelve men in the regiment between May and June 1864. Nine fell sick, including Sergeant James Dailey of Company D, a chronic asthmatic, and Private Stephen Love of Company B, stricken by measles. Diarrhea afflicted Henry Kirk, Matthew Lane, A. J. Pettigrew, and five other men. John McGough was laid low by pneumonia. Private Hurst must have had such losses in mind when he told his wife that "a great portion of the regiment has had to leave. The Regiment give out."[19]

Other men were "giving out" by quitting the army. One known deserter from the 66th, James Jolley, was an officer. Lieutenant Jolley had left Company B back in February for a thirty-day furlough in Bartow County. After the furlough expired, Nisbet received a certificate from a Bartow physician, asking for an extension of the leave. Nisbet refused and told Jolley to come back to camp. Jolley never returned. What ultimately happened to Jolley is unknown. Nisbet thought that Jolley deserted, and asked that his name be stricken from the muster rolls. "I believe he is affiliating with the enemy," Nisbet told one of Johnston's adjutants. Private Charles Smith of Company E left the regiment the same month, but by more conventional means: he was elected

---

[18] Nisbet, *Four Years*, 302–303.
[19] Hurst to wife, 20 June 1864, Hurst letters, KMNBP; CSRs for James S. Daley, Henry Kirk, Matthew P. Lane, Stephen Love, John McGough, and A. J. Pettigrew.

tax collector of Rabun County, an occupation exempt from conscription.[20]

Plenty of soldiers got out of the service, legally or not, in the other regiments in Walker's Division. Reports from the summer of 1864 make this clear. On the last day of April, Walker had 6,916 men present and 9,793 men total, both present and absent. Many of the latter were probably on detached duty, or absentees who returned once the campaign started. In the second week of June, the numbers rose to 8,100 and 13,616, respectively. By late June, Walker had 6,723 present and 13,331 total; two weeks later, there were 5,559 men still in the ranks, against a strength of 12,063 men on paper.[21] Walker's Division did not fight a single large battle during this time. Whence, then, went the thousands of absent soldiers? Doubtless some of Walker's losses were due to skirmishing. Doubtless, too, the oppressive heat, bad water, and constant marches broke down hundreds of soldiers. Even accounting for these factors, it seems that a large number of Walker's men deserted that summer.

After Kennesaw Mountain, the Army of Tennessee retreated to Smyrna, then to the banks of the Chattahoochee River. "We may remain here some time," Hurst wrote on 9 July from near the river. "Yet, [these are] very uncertain times." Sergeant Davis was sure that the army would retreat again. "Some think [the Yankees] can't flank us from the river," Davis told his wife, "but that is a mistake they will do it if they try." Twenty-four hours after the earlier letter, Hurst informed his wife, "last night our army was moved this side of the river." Once again, Sherman forced Johnston to fall back, by seizing river crossings downstream and sending part of his army over to threaten Johnston's right.

---

[20] Nisbet to A. P. Mason, 18 July 1864, James W. Jolley CSR; Charles E. Smith CSR.
[21] OR, vol. 38, pt. 3, pp. 676–79.

Johnston now had his back to Atlanta. "Atlanta is in great danger," Hurst decided. Sergeant Davis was in agreement: "We are a gone people without healp [sic] soon."[22]

Jefferson Davis was more disturbed than either Private Hurst or Sergeant Davis by what had happened. In his opinion, the desperate situation in Georgia was all Johnston's fault. Davis felt that the recalcitrant general spent too much time complaining about what he did not have, rather than creatively using what he did. Davis was especially furious when he learned that Johnston had fallen back across the Chattahoochee without a fight.[23]

Reviewing Johnston's constant retreats, Davis came to believe that Johnston would abandon Atlanta. Should that happen, the campaign would be a success for the North, ensuring Lincoln's reelection and shattering the Confederacy's hopes for victory. In a last-ditch effort, Davis telegraphed Johnston on 17 July, demanding that the general divulge his future plans. Johnston replied that he could only hope to win by fighting defensively, as he had thus far, but offered no concrete promise to fight for Atlanta. Dissatisfied with Johnston's proposed strategy, President Davis replaced him the next day with General John Bell Hood.[24]

"[Johnston's removal had] a strong impact on the army, and most of it negative," writes one historian. Many of Johnston's officers and men were saddened by his removal; some swore they would no longer fight. In Walker's Division, General Stevens was crestfallen. "The announcement that you are no longer to be our leader," Stevens informed Johnston, "was received by [this brigade] in silence and deep sorrow." As long as Johnston was in

---

[22] Hurst to wife, 9 and 10 July 1864 Hurst letters, KMNBP; Davis to wife, 6 July 1864, cited in Russell K. Brown, *To the Manner Born: The Life of General William H. T. Walker* (Athens: University of Georgia Press, 1994) 251.

[23] Castel, *Decision in the West*, 327–29, 344–47.

[24] Ibid., 360–61.

command, Stevens wrote, his soldiers had been confident of victory; "we [had] ever felt that the best was being done that could be." With Johnston gone, "our loss is irreparable."[25]

Several in the 66th Georgia were similarly upset that Johnston was removed. Colonel Nisbet recalled that, as they marched past Johnston in a final review, "some…broke ranks and grasped his hand, as the tears poured down their cheeks." Adjutant LeConte's postbellum account was inaccurate in the details—he dated the removal to mid-June, and claimed that Braxton Bragg had been put back in command—but likely quite accurate about the result: nearly every man in the regiment felt like crying at the news.[26]

After Johnston's removal, Confederate veterans and later historians debated the wisdom of the act and speculated about what might have happened if Johnston had stayed in command. Most upheld Johnston, arguing that he was steadily wearing down Sherman's army, and echoing Johnston's own postwar assertion that he could have held Atlanta "indefinitely."[27] Nisbet took this view in his memoirs. Relying heavily on Johnston's writings, Nisbet faulted President Davis for obstructing Johnston by withholding ammunition, artillery, and cavalry to raid against Sherman's supply lines and stop the Northern army. Nisbet also commended Johnston's leadership: "We knew that [he] had managed his campaign with skill. All that could be achieved, with

---

[25] Ibid., 363–65 (quote, 363); *OR,* vol. 38, pt. 4, pp. 890–91.

[26] Nisbet, *Four Years,* 308; LeConte, "Events of My Life," 21.

[27] For examples, see *Southern Historical Society Papers,* vol. 19 (1891; repr., Wilmington NC: Broadfoot Publishing Co., 1990) 354–63; Sam Watkins, *Company Aytch: A Sideshow of the Big Show* (New York: Collier Books, 1962) 125–30, 170–72 ; and William R. Scaife, *The Campaign for Atlanta* (Cartersville GA: Scaife Publications, 1993) especially 6–8 and 75–83. Johnston's defense of his operations can be found in *Battles and Leaders,* vol. 4 (New York: Castle Books, 1956) 260–77, and Joseph E. Johnston, *Narrative of Military Operations* (New York: D. Appleton and Co., 1874) 304–70.

the force and equipment he had, had been done. Flanked out of his positions, he had retreated with small loss of equipment and...*the un-impaired confidence of his army!... Johnston would have held Atlanta, and the Peace Party of the North would have triumphed, and the war would have come to a close then on some terms* [emphases original]."[28]

A few other accounts from the 66th Georgia suggest an ambiguous reaction to Johnston's removal. Lieutenant Briggs Napier, digging earthworks near Atlanta, was disappointed but not despondent. "[The removal] was a severe blow to the army," he told his girlfriend, "but I hope it may be for the best." William Hurst expected the worst, regardless of which general commanded the Army of Tennessee. "It seems to me that our country will finally be overrun by [Sherman's] army," Hurst confided to his wife in mid-July, "and we will be in a destitute condition no doubt." Sergeant Davis thought that the retreat from Dalton had long ago dashed hopes for victory: "if we could not hold them there we can't hold them no where." Even LeConte, who supported Johnston, thought that President Davis had good grounds for relieving the general, because Johnston had given up valuable territory, causing many Confederate soldiers to desert and allowing Sherman to get dangerously close to Atlanta.[29]

Regardless of how the men of the 66th Georgia felt about Johnston, they would have to get used to their new commander. Thirty-three years old, John Bell Hood was a pugnacious combat

---

[28] Nisbet, *Four Years*, 304–307.

[29] Napier to Bessie Reed, 19 July 1864, Napier Family Collection, Middle Georgia Archives; Hurst to Mary Hurst, 14 July 1864, Hurst Papers, KMNBP; Davis to Mary Davis, 9 July 1864, cited in Brown, *To the Manner Born,* 251; LeConte, "Events of My Life," 21. One historian of the Army of Tennessee found that men in late-war Confederate regiments tended to be more pessimistic about the outcome of the Atlanta Campaign, even during Johnston's tenure (Haughton, *Training, Tactics and Leadership,* 161–62).

leader who had earned his stripes in Virginia under Lee. Wounds at Gettysburg and Chickamauga had left Hood with a numb left arm and a missing right leg, but his ardor for battle remained undiminished. While recuperating in Richmond, Hood had gained the trust and friendship of President Davis, who sent him to the Army of Tennessee. During the Atlanta Campaign, Hood complained of Johnston's timidity in lengthy letters to Davis, suggesting that *he* would have done a better job. When Davis finally decided to replace Johnston, Hood seemed to be the best alternative.[30]

Two days after assuming command, Hood made his first attempt to drive Sherman away. In order to surround Atlanta, Sherman split his force to approach the city from three directions. McPherson's Army of the Tennessee moved east to Decatur and began wrecking the Georgia Railroad. Major General John M. Schofield, commanding the small Army of the Ohio, protected McPherson's right flank. The largest part of Sherman's army group, Major General George H. Thomas's Army of the Cumberland, 50,000 strong, moved directly south on Atlanta. Hood, determined to attack one of these isolated forces, selected Thomas's army as his target. Thomas's men had crossed sluggish, steep-banked Peach Tree Creek, north of Atlanta, but before they could entrench, two-thirds of Hood's army fell upon them on 20 July 1864.

The day of battle at Peach Tree Creek dawned hot; Federal soldiers in Thomas's army described the day as sultry and stifling. Nisbet's men would have been quite thirsty, for there were few streams in the area and the creek was in enemy hands. Their thirst would have been exacerbated by that morning's probable breakfast: salted beef and cornbread. Possibly they were quite

---

[30] Castel, *Decision in the West*, 75–78, 356–57; McMurry, *Atlanta 1864*, 94–95, 137–38.

tired, too. In a letter written a little more than a day before, Lieutenant Briggs Napier said that he and his men were busy "cutting trees for breastworks," an exhausting job normally, and especially so in the summer heat.[31] If that work had continued long into the night, as often happened in the Atlanta Campaign, the 66th Georgia would have awoken on 20 July sore and groggy. As noon approached, Nisbet and his officers likely sounded the assembly, inspected weapons, and then marched the regiment off to its place in the Confederate line, on the far left of Stevens's Brigade.[32] Stevens held the left of Walker's Division, in the center of General Hardee's corps.

Civil War soldiers believed that the most trying hours of battle were those right before the "ball opened." This was when the men on the battle line were alone with their thoughts, imagining all that might happen, hoping and praying for survival, wanting to fight well and do their duty—or, alternatively, trying to escape having to fight. For Nisbet's men, the waiting proved lengthy. Instead of marching out of their earthworks directly towards the enemy, they and their comrades in Hardee's Corps moved to the right. No sooner had they reached a position than they would be told to move again. Nisbet's men did not know that this maneuvering was due to reports that McPherson's men were advancing towards the city much quicker than expected as they wrecked the railroad. General Joseph Wheeler, the Confederate cavalry commander facing McPherson, became worried that the Federals might push through his thin lines that day. Hood thereupon ordered his entire army to shift right several miles, so that Wheeler might have some support against McPherson.[33]

---

[31] Robert Jenkins, e–mail, 23 July 2012; Briggs H. Napier to Bessie Reed, 19 July 1864, Napier Family Collection.

[32] Nisbet, *Four Years*, 307.

[33] Castel, *Decision in the West,* 371–73.

The rightward shift ended at 4:00 P.M., and the sun was already low in the sky when Hardee's four divisions finally advanced. Nisbet moved along the dusty Peachtree Road. It was well that Nisbet guided on the roadway, for wooded thickets, undergrowth, and deep ravines choked the ground before him. To facilitate movement in the tangled countryside, the regiment advanced in long columns, four-men wide.[34]

Hood's commanders did not have time to scout the area, relying on speed and surprise to carry their assaults. For the same reason, there were no skirmish lines ahead of the Confederate columns, which would have given a better understanding of the lay of the land and of enemy positions. Blind to what lay before them, Hardee's units became disoriented. To make matters worse, one of Hardee's divisions failed to advance alongside Walker and thereby left a gap on Nisbet's left flank. "I protested against advancing until this gap was filled," Nisbet wrote in his memoirs, "but the order was given—and the line went in."[35]

For perhaps one-quarter of a mile, Stevens's Brigade advanced without hindrance. Normally, they might have covered the distance in seven or eight minutes, moving at the "quick step" (80–90 yards a minute). Nisbet's men likely took far longer, stumbling over saplings and roots, detouring around large trees, and pulling through thick, clinging vines and briars. Near Peach Tree Creek, they began a slow, steady climb up to the crest of a low ridge.

Reaching the ridge top, the 66th Georgia came upon enemy skirmishers. A flurry of Yankee shots might have cut down a few of Nisbet's men, but within seconds the regiment overran the Federal rifle pits. Nisbet deployed into a two-rank line of battle. A short distance beyond the rifle pits, Nisbet's line finally tore

---

[34] Ibid., 375–76; Brown, *To the Manner Born*, 260; Nisbet, *Four Years*, 307.
[35] Castel, *Decision in the West*, 376; Nisbet, *Four Years*, 307.

through the underbrush and emerged into the open area around the Andrew Collier farm.

What Nisbet and his men saw at that moment must have dismayed them. Though Hood had supposedly promised that they would not have to attack trenches, Nisbet's soldiers faced a line of barricades in front of Union General Nathan Kimball's brigade.[36] Fashioned from logs, sticks, stones, fence rails, and knapsacks, these barricades were meant to absorb a few bullets and encourage the Federals to fire low and, thus, more accurately.[37] Nisbet's men emerged from the woods so quickly that Kimball's Federals had to throw down their axes and shovels to fight. Halting, the 66th Georgia leveled rifles and fired simultaneously with the Federals.[38] Initial volleys at close range were often devastating, but in this case, most of the Confederate bullets probably flew harmlessly overhead or buried deep in the barricades, while many of the Federal bullets likely found the mark. Nisbet probably suffered his heaviest losses at this time.[39]

Helplessly exposed, Nisbet's men dropped at an alarming rate. Fifty-eight-caliber bullets and shotgun-like blasts of canister from six artillery pieces shattered the left leg of William Hudgins and the right leg of Thomas Massengale, tore the shoulder of Captain Lorenzo Belisle, plowed into the skull of James Atcherson, and felled others by the dozen. After a few minutes, those still standing must have sought cover behind trees or on the slope of the ridge.

---

[36] Nisbet *Four* Years, 312. Most of Thomas's line was in the open; Kimball's brigade was one of the few units to entrench (Castel, *Decision in the West*, 380–83).

[37] Ibid., 372–73.

[38] Ibid., 376.

[39] Robert D. Jenkins, Sr., *The Battle of Peachtree Creek: Hood's First Sortie* (Macon GA: Mercer University Press, 2014).

As badly wounded soldiers writhed around on the ground, and others made for the rear, the regiment slowly bled away.[40]

To the credit of their bravery, the men of the 66th Georgia kept trying to take position with repeated attacks all along the line after the initial assault had failed. Lieutenant Ross mentioned a couple of sorties that afternoon; "we charged the Yankee breastworks twice," he told his mother. Small groups of Nisbet's soldiers, led by stalwart company officers or brave enlisted men, may have darted from tree to tree while firing—or more likely, given the regiment's inexperience, rushed forward *en masse* with fixed bayonets. At the head of one attack, the wounded Captain Belisle, his arm useless and bleeding, got within 20 yards of the Federal line before he was struck a second time, in the groin, and fell down in agony. The reckless audacity of Belisle and his fellow Confederates was for naught: each attack was shot.[41]

Repulsed, the 66th Georgia sprawled on the slope of the ridge, bloodied and coming apart on the left under an enfilading fire. Eventually, General Stevens rode to Nisbet's position, saw that the men could not make any headway, and told Nisbet to fall back. Seconds later, Stevens's horse was killed, and as the general struggled out of the saddle, he was hit behind the left ear by a Federal bullet. Nisbet told Lieutenant Napier and Captain Charles Williamson to carry the mortally wounded Stevens to a hospital, then ordered a withdrawal. Napier, Williamson, and maybe many others were shot as the regiment pulled out.[42]

---

[40] Ibid.; Lorenzo Belisle pension application, 1889, Georgia Confederate Pension Applications, Coweta County; W. P. Hudgins pension application, 1889, GCPA, Dekalb County; Thomas J. Massengale pension application, 1889, GCPA, Jones County; James Atcherson CSR.

[41] *OR*, vol. 38, pt. 1, pp. 306, 321; Ross to mother, 25 July 1864, NBRR Collection, Middle Georgia Archives; Belisle pension application, GCPA.

[42] Nisbet, *Four Years*, 307–308; Brown, *To the Manner Born*, 261.

Peach Tree Creek had been a defeat for Hood, who lost 2,500 of his men to Thomas's 1,500 causalties. Many factors combined to frustrate the Army of Tennessee that day, not the least of which was bad luck. To many Confederates, the root cause of their defeat was Hood. Others recognized that the plan had been sound, but its execution had been sloppy. "[The attack] succeeded admirably in every portion of the line," one of Stevens's men wrote, "except with Walker's…Division, [which] failed to carry the Yankee works—on account of *bad generalship*" (emphasis original).[43]

The battle took a serious toll on the 66th. Nisbet estimated after the war that his regiment lost 25 percent of all men engaged. Lieutenant Ross, five days after the battle, put the casualties closer to 50 percent. "We went into the fight with 190 men," Ross told his mother, "& lost 74."[44] The regiment's roster offers entirely different numbers. Fifty-four men—fourteen killed, thirty-six wounded, and four captured—were known to have been casualties at Peach Tree Creek.[45] Beyond exact losses, the number of men on duty according to Ross poses an additional question: what had happened to the once-oversized 66th Georgia? After accounting for all attrition from April 1863 to July 1864, the 66th ought to

---

[43] Castel, *Decision in the West,* 381; Robert G. Mitchell to wife, 23 July 1864, Robert G. Mitchell Papers, Special Collections, UGA.

[44] Nisbet, *Four Years,* 308; Ross to mother, 25 July 1864, NBRR Collection, Middle Georgia Archives. There is one other estimate of the regiment's strength which might be closer to the truth than Ross's estimate. Edgar A. Ross, the lieutenant's brother, wrote that the 66th Georgia had "four hundred and eighty" men at hand on 20 July. Unfortunately, Edgar Ross did not offer a source for this number, "Early History of the Luke Ross Family in Georgia," BNRR Collection.

[45] Henderson, *Roster,* vol. 4, 693–771. After careful research, Robert Jenkins has counted eighty-one casualties incurred by the 66th Georgia on 20 July, Jenkins, e-mail, 23 July 2012.

have had at least 800 men in the ranks at Peach Ttree Creek.[46] The records do show that 104 men were sick, 42 were absent without leave, 7 had deserted and 5 were arrested in late summer 1864. However, these losses were from July to August. Even if every single man in question was missing before 20 July, the 66th Georgia still should have numbered between 650 and 700.

Apart from other, undocumented combat losses that spring and summer, the 66th Georgia must have had more deserters; known losses from desertion for this time—four or five men—are probably far too low. Yet desertion cannot account for all of the missing men above. If Georgia soldiers tended to quit the army when their home counties were invaded by Federal soldiers, that would not explain why so many left the 66th Georgia when most of their homes, in the Plantation Belt, were not threatened.[47] Furthermore, if the regiment lost almost 500 men to desertion—a staggering 75 percent of its strength—during this period, one would expect some mention of it in the letters from Privates Davis and Hurst or Lieutenants Napier and Ross. None of these men spoke of a higher-than-average level of desertion.

A letter from Hurst, placed in context, offers one possible explanation why the 66th Georgia was so tiny when it fought at Peach Tree Creek: "We have seen hard times… Our rashings [sic] have been light and we have been exposed very much in the rain… We have had but little time to sleep or rest since last Wednesday and don't know when we will have… *A great portion of the regiment has had to leave. The Regiment give out*" (emphases original).[48] Hurst did not say the men were quitting because they were sick of the war and wanted to go home. Instead, "light

---

[46] This assumes that *all* sick, wounded and absent men during the period remained so.

[47] For the specifics of this argument, see Weitz, "A Higher Duty," 106–55.

[48] Hurst to wife, 20 June 1864, Hurst letters, KMNBP.

rashings," exposure, rain, and lack of sleep were to blame. The result? "The Regiment give out." Hurst's comrades did not necessarily *want* to leave, but they *had to*. Generally older and thus less hardy, their bodies could not bear the hardships of camp and campaign as well as younger soldiers.[49] If Hurst was right, then the 66th Georgia had suffered an alarming physical breakdown; it would need time to recuperate before entering battle again.

Unfortunately, rest was unavailable, for Sherman still threatened Atlanta. A new Confederate plan was necessary, and it took Hood only a day to come up with one. He would strike again at Sherman's divided forces, this time at McPherson's Army of the Tennessee. Confederate cavalry reported on 21 July that McPherson was still separated from Thomas and Schofield, and that McPherson's left flank was "in the air," unprotected by reserves or a natural barrier. Hood decided to execute a bold flank attack, by sending Hardee's Corps through Atlanta, southeast along the McDonough Road, and then northeast to Decatur, to get around and behind McPherson. After Hardee had crumpled up McPherson's flank, another Confederate corps under General Cheatham would strike McPherson in the front.[50]

For this to work, Hardee's Corps would have to march 15 to 20 miles in eight hours through the night of the 21st and then attack McPherson at dawn on the 22nd. First though, Hardee's men first had to fall back from Peach Tree Creek. Nisbet, appointed officer of the day for Walker's Division, was responsible for withdrawing Walker's picket posts. Worried that, if he issued a general withdrawal order, some Confederate deserter might betray the news to the other side, Nisbet crept along the picket line from

---

[49] Kenneth W. Noe, *Reluctant Rebels: The Confederates who Joined the Army After 1861* (Chapel Hill: University of North Carolina Press, 2010) 195, 206.

[50] Gary Ecelbarger, *The Day Dixie Died: The Battle of Atlanta* (New York: Thomas Dunne Books, 2010) 49–50.

outpost to outpost, passing the word himself. In the darkness, the young colonel accidentally stepped on a rotten stick, alerting a nearby Yankee picket who fired towards the sound. Nisbet barely dodged the bullet and drew his revolver to fire back, but, not wanting to draw any further attention, he crept away silently and rejoined his regiment.[51]

Ahead of the 66th Georgia lay a long night march—the kind most detested by soldiers. Hardee's Corps quickly became strung out as soldiers stopped, started, and stopped again. Absolute darkness played havoc on the marching column: toes and heels were stepped on, knees and shins were scraped against fence rails, and eyes and noses were snapped by low-hanging branches. Dust and heat only increased the Confederates' thirst. Exhaustion from the march compounded exhaustion from the past two months of campaigning. Many men in the 66th Georgia and other regiments dropped out along the way.[52]

Straggling and weariness completely upset Hood's timetable; it was not until 11:30 A.M. on 22 July, that Hardee's Corps finally deployed, and advanced into battle. Once again, as at Peach Tree Creek, Walker's Division was broken up by the terrain. Thick woods, ravines, and a steep-banked stream, Sugar Creek, cut off most of Stevens's Brigade from the 66th Georgia. Nisbet himself was separated from the neighboring brigade of Brigadier General States Right Gist.[53] Nisbet's target was a six-gun Federal battery, the 14th Ohio Light, on a hill to his right center.[54] A brigade of Federals supporting the battery was shooting a Confederate assault to pieces. To make a frontal attack would be suicidal, so Nisbet

---

[51] Nisbet, *Four Years*, 308–309.
[52] Ecelbarger, *The Day Dixie Died,* 60–61, 62–63.
[53] Ibid., 67–69, 85–86.
[54] Nisbet, *Four Years*, 310–11.

followed the bed of Sugar Creek north, hoping to find a crossing site and take the battery from the rear.

In that moment, Nisbet must have realized that things were not going according to plan. Instead of an unprotected Federal flank, Hardee's Corps ran into opposition. Hardee and his subordinates could not have known that McPherson suspecting an attack, had adjusted his position to cover the endangered area.[55] Hardee's men would somehow have to overcome their utter exhaustion and punch through McPherson's lines. They would also have to take care not to endanger their own flanks. Nisbet was very concerned about the latter possibility. Gist's Brigade had fallen behind Nisbet, and so a yawning gap had opened on the left of the 66th Georgia. Remembering the damage done to his regiment by a similar failure at Peach Tree Creek, Nisbet begged for support. None would be forthcoming; Hardee's forces were already engaged and there were no reserves to spare. With a sense of foreboding, Nisbet divided the 66th Georgia into three "wings," taking personal command of the left wing.[56]

Tired, isolated, and under strength, the men of the 66th Georgia stumbled through the marshy underbrush. They had every reason to feel jumpy. Earlier that morning, as Walker's Division had deployed in an overgrown field, a few Federal skirmishers behind a split-rail fence had nearly put a bullet through Nisbet's head. The colonel threw himself to the ground, and the shots killed Lieutenant John Rogers of Company A instead. Rogers had been very popular, and his death deflated the regiment's spirits. Some men who saw Rogers fall mistook him for

---

[55] The force protecting McPherson's flank was the four-brigade XVI Corps. Coincidentally, these were the same Federals that Nisbet had opposed at Snake Creek Gap on 9 May.

[56] Nisbet, *Four Years*, 310–11.

Nisbet, and word spread that the colonel was dead.[57] The regiment's morale became even more shaky.

A little after 1:00 P.M., the 66th Georgia approached the foot of the hill where the 14th Ohio Light Artillery was positioned. There were only 110 men present; the rest had fallen out during the march.[58] Nisbet halted the regiment, adjusted its line, and prepared to cross a cleared field ahead. Suddenly, a long line of men in blue arose from hiding, and there was an explosion of gunfire. Nisbet cried, "Charge!" and ran into the field. The enemy advanced as well. It was all over within seconds, as soon as Nisbet found himself "surrounded...by a great number [of Federal soldiers]...all exclaiming, 'You are my prisoner!'" The colonel looked back. Only ten men had followed him; the rest of the 66th Georgia had disappeared. Nisbet stood still and said nothing, but for him the war was over. He was now in the hands of the Union Army.[59]

Nisbet had been surprised by the Yankees, but the Yankees had not been surprised by him. General John Fuller, one of McPherson's generals, had seen the 66th Georgia and realized that it would enter a gap in his lines. Fuller sent two regiments, the 27th and 39th Ohio, to plug the gap and repulse Nisbet. The Ohioans had been given orders to lie down in the field, wait until the 66th Georgia was halfway across, then rise up, fire a volley and charge. In that way, the Federals might capture most or all of the Confederates before they could retreat into the woods. To Fuller's regret, his Buckeyes bungled the assignment by firing on the 66th Georgia the minute it appeared. After a short fight, the rest of the

[57] Ibid., 311–12; John H. Rogers CSR. Nisbet's family was also mistakenly informed that he had been killed, ibid.

[58] William R. Ross to mother, 25 July 1864, BNRR Collection, Middle Georgia Archives.

[59] Nisbet, *Four Years*, 311–312.

Georgians ran off into the woods, safe from pursuit. Fuller had to be content with the capture of Nisbet, plus "1 captain, 1 adjutant, and 13 men."[60]

Actually, Fuller was mistaken about capturing Adjutant LeConte. That officer claimed to have followed Nisbet into the field. Under "a perfect hail of Minnie balls, spherical case and shrapnel" (in reality, the regiment never came under Federal artillery fire), LeConte's contingent faltered and dropped down behind some stumps for cover. As LeConte tried to roust his company forward, he was shot. The bullet clipped a nerve near his leg, crumpling LeConte to the ground. Nisbet ordered LeConte to the rear, and with great exertion and in considerable pain, the adjutant limped away.[61]

Only a small part of the 66th Georgia followed Nisbet in the charge on 22 July. Why was the regiment not there when Nisbet needed them most? Why did they not try to rescue him from the Federals? One possible explanation is that Nisbet's men hated him and were glad to be rid of him. This seems unlikely. None of the regiment's letter writers expressed a dislike for Nisbet, and none mentioned any hard feelings against Nisbet amongst the rank and file. Nisbet probably had some detractors, but there is no evidence that the 66th Georgia would have welcomed his death, wounding or capture. Another possible explanation is that Nisbet's men saw their commander charge, but were unable or unwilling to follow. It must be remembered that they were incredibly tired, hot, thirsty, and nervous. They might not have had the energy to save their colonel. They might have preferred to wait for the Yankees to approach and then blast them from the safety of the woods. Perhaps, too, the action took place so quickly that Nisbet was captured before the 66th Georgia could react. Finally, it could be

[60] *OR*, vol. 38, pt. 3, pp. 475–76, 502.
[61] LeConte, "Events of My Life," 22–23.

that most of Nisbet's men were elsewhere. While Nisbet led one wing, the other two wings might have gotten lost and gone in another direction. It might be that those who were captured or killed alongside Nisbet were the only ones who saw what happened.

While Nisbet's regiment withdrew and Nisbet was led off into captivity, the battle continued. Walker's Division was repulsed, and the general was shot dead. "I tied [Walker's] handkerchief around his chin when we brought Him off the field," Lieutenant Ross claimed after the battle. "Poor man he was so wicked." To Walker's left, Cleburne's Division tore into McPherson's lines, killing McPherson, and rolling up the left flank of a Federal corps. Later in the afternoon, Cheatham's corps entered the fray, punched through the left center of the Federal line, routed several brigades and captured two artillery batteries. McPherson's Federals, however, were eager to avenge the death of their beloved commander, and they would not be denied victory. Eventually, they rallied and recaptured the lost guns and ground. "Our loss is heavy," Ross told his mother, "but we have badly crippled the enemy." Other Confederate soldiers shared Ross's view, claiming victory in the Battle of Atlanta. In truth, Hood had lost again, at a cost of more than 5,000 Confederates.[62]

Fifty-eight men in the 66th were put out of action on 22 July according to Ross, thirty-seven according to the regiment's roster. If Ross was correct, then the regiment had lost 70 percent of its strength in just two days. Even the more conservative numbers from the roster amount to almost 40 percent total casualties. Many regiments in the Army of Tennessee had suffered as badly as the 66th Georgia, and a few had suffered worse. "The fine army of

[62] Ross to mother, 25 July 1864, BNRR Collection; Brown, *To the Manner Born*, 271–75; Castel, *Decision in the West*, 395–414; Daniel, *Soldiering in the Army of Tennessee*, 149; Ecelbarger, *The Day Dixie Died*, 96–97.

General Joe Johnston was thus decimated," Nisbet wrote many years later, "without any beneficial results."[63]

Of the 66th's chroniclers, Sergeant James Crane and Lieutenant Ross escaped these battles untouched. Private William Hurst and Sergeant John Davis did not. The former was killed at Peach Tree Creek. James Hurst reassured his sister-in-law that, "[William's] motto was death before dishonor, so he died the death of a Christian and a patriot. I wish we could all live and die in the right as he has." Sergeant Davis was also among the casualties at Peach Tree Creek. "I was wounded in a charge on the 20th," the sergeant wrote his wife from a hospital in Griffin, "the Ball entered my left side just below the ribs and ranged down struck the hip bone glanced around the back bone thare [sic]." Fearing that his wound might become fatally infected, Davis urged his wife to send his father to the hospital with a carriage, so that he might come home to his family for the end.[64]

Lieutenant Napier was going home as well. Shot in the leg while trying to carry off General Stevens's body, the lieutenant had almost been left to die near Peach Tree Creek before being rescued by his girlfriend's brother, a soldier in the 63rd Georgia Infantry. In a field hospital, doctors examined Napier's leg and determined that it would have to be amputated. Napier did not agree; "he wanted to go to the grave all together," so much so that the surgeon had to take away Napier's pistol in order to safely operate. The lieutenant was brought back to his parents' house in Bibb County to recuperate. Napier later had a second operation, which, as he told Bessie, "so much reduced me that I was very near

---

[63] Nisbet, *Four Years*, 315.
[64] James Hurst to Matilda Hurst, undated, Hurst letters, KMNBP; John M. Davis to wife, 3 August 1864, Civil War Miscellany, GDAH.

passing to that place whence no traveler returns," but at least he was alive.[65]

Company and squad commanders like Napier and Davis were the glue that helped hold the 66th Georgia together; their absence weakened the regiment. Aside from its captured colonel and its crippled adjutant, the 66th Georgia had lost eighteen officers and thirteen non-commissioned officers. Six companies—A, C, D, G, H, and K—were now without their captains, joining a seventh (B), without a captain since Resaca. Twelve lieutenants were dead or wounded. Lieutenant Colonel Hamilton, now the ranking officer, had missed the battles due to severe diarrhea. Major Hull, the new second-in-command, had been wounded at Peach Tree Creek. That left Captain Thomas Langston of Company K in charge of the regiment, except Langston had also been wounded at Peach Tree Creek.[66] The 66th Georgia had become critically short of officers.

An inspection report of Stevens's Brigade from mid-August came to the same conclusion. Lieutenant F. M. Stafford, the inspecting officer, found just 144 men in the 66th Georgia present for duty, and 108 actually on the firing line, with 104 serviceable weapons. A mere eleven men had all the necessary accoutrements (cartridge boxes, cap pouches, bayonet scabbards, and shoulder and waist belts), and half of the regiment was without pants or drawers. The men were short of socks, blankets, knapsacks and

---

[65]Briggs H. Napier Reminisces, Civil War Miscellany, GDAH; Napier to Bessie Reed, 1 November 1864, Briggs H. Napier Family Collection, Middle Georgia Archives.

[66]CSRs for Algernon S. Hamilton, Robert N. Hull, and Thomas L. Langston.

haversacks, and they were entirely without shoes.[67] It was a sad picture of a once-proud unit.

Stafford gave the regiment high marks for "Military Bearing," "Discipline," and "Drill," but classified them "indifferent" in regards to "Military Appearance." The lieutenant also noted that the 66th was not "clean" and did not police its camps very well. Reviewing Stevens's entire command, Stafford wrote: "[*Their*] *present condition…is not good, having suffered very heavily during the existing Campaign, especially in Officers…* I regret to state that *a good many desertions are occurring,* owing I think to the demoralization in the Command consequent to its heavy losses in battle, the want of…Shoes and clothing…*and the need of good Officers…* (emphases added).[68]

Two figures given in this report deserve attention. The first is the regiment's sick list. In stark proof of Private Hurst's assertion that the regiment "gave out," there are 25 officers and 253 enlisted men absent from illness. This is double the losses from sickness documented in the regimental roster for July and August. Fifty-eight of the sick men appear in the census records. Nineteen were in their mid-twenties or younger, the ideal age for a soldier, but almost all the rest were thirty or older, and close to half were older than forty.

The second figure of note is the number of men "absent without authority": eighty-nine. Once again, the number is double that gleaned from the roster. Twenty-one of the absentees can be found in the census records. They include five teenagers, three men in their twenties, five men in their thirties, and eight men (one-third of the total) in their forties. C. W. Bruce, an overseer,

---

[67]Inspection Report of Jackson's Brigade, Bate's Division, Army of Tennessee, 17 August 1864, Inspection Reports and Related Records, record group 109, War Department Collection of Confederate Records, NARA.
[68]Ibid.

and H. J. Summers, a carpenter, stand out amongst twelve farmers and farmhands and seven men without occupations. Half of the absentees were married with children, the other half were single and living at home, not counting widower Benjamin James of Company I. Thirteen of the twenty-one absentees held no assets. If their poverty, and perhaps a few distressing letters from home, caused them to quit the ranks, the same cannot be said of corporals R. F. G. Roberts and John Odell and Private Stephen Brown, who were among the regiment's wealthier men. Maybe these three slipped out of the lines around Atlanta in late summer 1864 in order to enjoy a bit of the good life that they had left behind. Fourteen of the twenty-one eventually returned; five of those who returned later died in the service.[69]

Privates Jourdan Bridger, Thomas Haynes, James Henderson, and Berry Hicks would not return. They were part of seven men, all from Company B, who deserted from the regiment at Atlanta. Apart from their meager means—$450 in property between them—they were a disparate group. Bridger, a miller and a married father, was the oldest at forty-eight; farmer Hicks, also married with children, was the second oldest at thirty-seven; and Haynes (married) and Henderson (single) were both in their mid-twenties.

In his inspection report, Lt. Stafford faulted the officers of the 66th Georgia for not properly instructing their men in picket duty. Stafford might have been thinking about what had happened to the regiment in early August. Following a third Confederate defeat at Ezra Church (28 July 1864), Hood pulled back into the trenches around Atlanta, and the siege of the city began. There were skirmishes, probes and trench raids nearly every day, as both sides jockeyed for position.

---

[69]Ibid.

During a lull in the fighting, on 7 August, Lieutenant Ross, in command of the regiment's skirmish line, sat down and tried to finish a letter to his fiancée, Emma Jane Kennon. Halfway through, the lieutenant switched from a pen to a pencil, because: "One of my men just turned over my bottle of ink. He is Excusable, however, for the Yankees are shelling us pretty considerably and in attempting to dodge a shell my ink went up. It is really amusing to see what effect noise of shells produces upon some men, in fact...I acknowledge that I will dodge them myself...."[70]

Ross never finished writing, for in a minute, a cluster of Yankees swarmed up out of the ground, rushed across the "no man's land" between the opposing armies, and fallen upon the outposts of the 66th Georgia. After a brief fight, the attackers, part of the 14th Michigan Infantry, captured the fell, along with eight of Ross's men. Three wounded Georgians managed to get away, but three others lay on the ground, dead or soon to become so. Walking over to them, a Federal officer, Major Thomas Fitzgibbon, noticed that one of the stricken men was a lieutenant.

A week later, Emma received two letters. One, from Ross, was soaked in blood. The other letter, written by Major Fitzgibbon and sent through the lines, told her that Ross was no more. Hit by a bullet in his spinal cord, the young lieutenant "retained his reason to the last, but sobbed bitterly as he directed me to take your likeness from his breast pocket." "From his dying lips," Fitzgibbon told Emma, "he told me he loved you above all else in the world."[71]

---

[70]Ross to Emma Jane Kennon, 6 August 1864, BNRR Collection, Middle Georgia Archives.

[71] *Leavenworth Daily Times,* 9 September 1864; "Battlefield Letters to Mother and Sweetheart," *Atlanta Journal*, 25 April 1943, 8–9.

The men of the 66th Georgia must have wondered whether the loss of Ross and so many others was in vain, for their sacrifices—and those of the rest of the Army of Tennessee—did not save Atlanta. When the month-long siege, punctuated by artillery bombardments, failed to drive out Hood, Sherman decided to make Atlanta untenable by cutting the last of its rail lines. In late August, Sherman moved most of his force to the west and then south, toward the Macon & Western Railroad. Hood countered with two of his corps, under General Hardee, at Jonesboro, hoping that they could stop Sherman, but in a two-day battle (31 August–1 September 1864), Hood's men suffered defeat a fourth time and the railroad fell into Federal hands. No longer able to supply his army or protect Atlanta, Hood retreated to the southeast as Sherman's armies entered the city on 2 September.

The 66th Georgia joined in the retreat. It had lost twenty-three men at Jonesboro, among them two privates, George Lee and John Mooney, who during the battle had deserted to the Federals.[72] Only a year after it had left Macon for its first campaign, the 66th Georgia seemed to be losing the will to fight. Atlanta was lost, the 66th Georgia had been badly beaten in combat, and Colonel Nisbet was no longer there to guide his men. Everything had gone wrong. Was the future going to be any brighter? Many, perhaps most, of the men in the regiment believed it would, or at least hoped it would. Others reflecting on the campaign must have wondered whether the final curtain was about to come down.

---

[72] CSRs for George W. Lee and Jonathan Mooney.

Chapter 6

To Tennessee and Back:
The Last Campaigns and the Post-War World

"I have passed through the dangers of battle safely," Sergeant James Crane of the 66th Georgia assured his parents in Athens, "and now am sitting quietly in the shade writing as if I had never known what war was." Crane, who had fought at Jonesboro, was fortunate to have come through untouched except for a small contusion on his knee. Another man, Private James Street of Company C, one of the regiment's eleven wounded in the battle, would lose his leg, and then his life, later that fall.[1] There was some consolation in that plenty of Yankees had also been killed at Jonesboro; a few of Crane's comrades had been over to see their graves. Still, many more Yankees were in Atlanta, and Crane feared they might march to Athens and wreak havoc on the city. Crane wanted to be nearby to protect his parents. Thankfully for him, the Army of Tennessee remained where it was for the moment. "We have established a regular camp," Crane wrote, "and expect to stay some time as we were ordered to fix up bunks."[2]

The regiment's time near Jonesboro would be shorter than Crane expected, for General Hood had a new plan to thwart the Federal forces in Georgia. After losing Atlanta, Hood had retreated

---

[1] Crane to family, 10 and 14 September 1864; James W. Street compiled service record (CSR), National Archives and Records Administration (NARA), Washington, DC (All CSR citations are for the 66th Georgia Infantry unless otherwise noted.).

[2] Ibid.

to Lovejoy Station, southeast of the city, but had not given up his hope of defeating Sherman. Now freed from having to protect a fixed point, Hood believed that he could march wherever he pleased, and he intended to sever Sherman's supply lines. Two or three weeks of tearing up railroads, burning depots, and capturing garrisons would draw Sherman away from Atlanta lest his army starve. President Davis, who had traveled west to visit the Army of Tennessee, approved the plan.

On the last day of September, Hood's forces, down to 40,000 men, crossed the Chattahoochee River and headed north. Losses around Atlanta had led to many organizational changes. In Hardee's Corps, now under General Cheatham, the Georgia division of slain General Walker had suffered such heavy casualties that it had been disbanded, its brigades transferred to other divisions. The brigade formerly under General Stevens, also dead, was now commanded by another Georgian, Brigadier General Henry R. Jackson, in the division of Major General William B. Bate.[3]

Like other brigades in the Army of Tennessee, Jackson's was small in numbers, totaling little more than 700 men. Its original five regiments had been consolidated into three regiments and a battalion. One of the consolidated units was the 66th Georgia, now combined with the 1st Georgia Infantry. The two regiments together had 267 men present for duty in mid-September, but there is no way to know how many were originally from the 66th.[4]

When Lieutenant Stafford inspected the brigade that month, many earlier problems were still evident. The 1st/66th Georgia remained short of clothes and accoutrements, and more than 600 men were either sick or absent without leave. On the other hand,

[3] Castel, *Decision in the West*, 198, 552.

[4] Inspection Report, Jackson's brigade, Bate's division, Army of Tennessee, 17 September 1864, Inspection Reports and Related Records, RG 109, NARA.

the consolidated regiment did not have a single black mark in its efficiency ratings, and desertion had almost entirely ceased. "The General Condition and discipline [of Jackson's brigade]," Stafford concluded, "has improved very much."[5]

Seven men from the 66th Georgia, stayed behind when the Army of Tennessee left Jonesboro. Four of them—Privates Columbus Alford, George Davis, Matthew Lane, and S. M. Thomas—can be found in the census records. They were quite poor, owning less than $1,250 in property combined, yet it does not follow that they were deserting "a rich man's war." Alford, Lane and Thomas were in bad health—Thomas, for example, had been sick in fall 1863, winter 1864, and the following summer—and Davis had been wounded at Peach Tree Creek. The war might go on, but their bodies could not take any more. All seven men joined state troops hastily assembled to protect Macon and other Georgia cities.[6]

Throughout the early fall, Hood and Sherman marched across North Georgia, Hood heading northwest, Sherman in hot pursuit. Hood's men tore up the Western & Atlantic Railroad, stabbed at Sherman's supply depots, and captured a few isolated Federal units, but accomplished little else. Hood found out that he could not starve Sherman out of Georgia this way, for Federal rail crews quickly repaired the damage done. Nearly cornered near Chattanooga, the Confederate commander ducked west into Alabama and rethought his options.

Hood soon formulated another plan, as characteristically bold as the last. He would invade and liberate Tennessee. If Sherman came after him, all the better; Georgia would be freed of Yankees, and Sherman's army might be destroyed. If Sherman stayed in

---

[5] Ibid.

[6] See CSRs for Columbus G. Alford, George W. Davis, Matthew P. Lane, and S. M. Thomas.

Georgia, Hood could push into Kentucky, then head north all the way to the Ohio River, and perhaps beyond. The Midwest would be thrown into a panic; the North would have to divert other forces after Hood; and Virginia—where Lee's Army of Northern Virginia was now besieged at Petersburg—would be relieved. Maybe Lincoln would be forced to sue for peace.

This plan, born of desperation and devoid of any real chance of success, was almost shattered before it could fairly begin. First, there were logistical problems. Hood's raid into North Georgia had failed to cut off Sherman's supplies, but it had completely cut off Hood from his own. In Alabama, the Army of Tennessee scrambled to assemble food and fodder, but was frustrated by worn-out railroads, a shortage of draft animals, and Hood's own incompetent administration. Second, the weather turned bad in early November. Rains fell for week after week, postponing invasion.[7]

Finally, getting over the Tennessee River in Alabama was a dangerous enough. Federal gunboats patrolled long stretches of the river, and strong Federal garrisons held key crossing sites. Hood first tried to cross at Guntersville, close to the Georgia state line, but was forced to shift several miles west to Decatur. Here, 3,000 Yankee soldiers, heavily entrenched, stood guard. Hood carefully moved his army toward the town on 27 October, taking advantage of a ravine to shelter a sudden rush against the Federal trenches. Alerted, the Federals sallied out the next day, trapped some of Hood's men in the ravine, and inflicted over 150 casualties. The 66th Georgia was especially hard hit in the action, losing two officers—Lieutenants M. B. F. Helms and James Hendon—six non-commissioned officers and twenty-seven

[7] Wiley Sword, *Embrace an Angry Wind: The Confederacy's Last Hurrah—Spring Hill, Franklin and Nashville* (New York: Harper Collins, 1992) 65–74.

enlisted men killed, wounded, or captured. Rebuffed, Hood again moved west in search of an easier crossing site.[8]

It was not until mid-November that the Army of Tennessee was ready to go. While Sherman, set out from Atlanta on his famed, destructive "March to the Sea," Hood's men crossed the Tennessee River on pontoon boats at Florence, Alabama. "We [went]…with colors flying and bands playing," Sergeant Crane yold to his father. The citizens of Florence turned out to see the Army of Tennessee, but although Crane appreciated the their show of support, he had grave doubts about their Confederate patriotism: "The ladies were all out…waving their handkerchiefs and appearing to be very glad to see us, while at the same time they had on Yankee goods[,] Fine furs and silks purchased in Nashville."[9]

On 21 November, the Army of Tennessee began to enter its namesake state. It faced a large number of Federal soldiers, under the command of General George H. Thomas, but the Federal units were scattered. Hood hoped to interpose his men between the separate parts of the Federal army, cut them off from Nashville, and capture the city. Approaching the town of Columbia, about 40 miles south of Nashville, Hood encountered 23,000 Federals under General John M. Schofield. To trap the Federals, Hood had one corps of his army hold Schofield's attention and swung the other two corps around the Federal flank. Hood's objective was the village of Spring Hill, northeast of Columbia along the road to Nashville. If Hood seized the town, Schofield would be isolated from Thomas and ultimately destroyed.

Initially, Hood's plan worked well. While Schofield remained inert near Columbia, Confederate cavalry under General Nathan

---

[8] Ibid., 64–65; CSRs for M. B. F. Nelms and James W. Hendon.
[9] Crane to family, 17 November 1864, Crane letters, AHC.

Bedford Forrest screened Hood's flanking movement. Hard marching on 29 November brought Hood's flanking corps, including Bate's Division and the 66th Georgia, reached Spring Hill by late afternoon. Only a small contingent of Federal soldiers held the town, and Hood deployed his forces to capture them. Bate's Division took the far left of the Confederate line and pushed forward to seize the Columbia Pike, but just as they. Just as Bate's men neared the road, they were ordered to withdraw and support other Confederate units.[10]

Hood believed that he had cut off Schofield's retreat and went to bed early, expecting that his army would soon attack and seal the victory. While Hood slept, his generals became confused, argued with each other, and refused to coordinate their actions. No attack was ever launched, and when darkness set in, the army went into camp. All the while, Schofield, conscious of the trap laid for him, led his men on a stealthy march through Spring Hill—right past Hood's army. At times the Federal units were within sight of the Confederate pickets, none of whom raised the alarm. As day broke, Schofield had already slipped through Hood's grasp.[11]

When Hood awoke on 30 November to find that the Army of Tennessee had failed to bag Schofield, he was, in the words of an aide, "wrathy as a rattlesnake." Angered and humiliated, Hood ordered an immediate pursuit. Later that day at Franklin, 10 miles north of Spring Hill, the Federals were cornered behind imposing fortifications. Hood ordered a frontal attack, aiming to drive the Federals into the nearby Harpeth River before they could reach the safety of Nashville.[12] Seven divisions of Confederate infantry, 20,000 strong, advanced across two miles of open ground towards

[10] Sword, *Embrace an Angry Wind,* 124–27, 135–39.
[11] Ibid., 140–55.
[12] Ibid., 156–57, 177–80.

Schofield's earthworks. Bate's men were on the far left of the
Army of Tennessee, with Jackson's Brigade in the center of the
division. Under a fierce fire, the Georgians clawed through a thick
grove of locust trees and came within a stone's throw of the
Federal line. Too few to take and hold the trenches, they fell
back.[13] The story was much the same for the rest of the Army of
Tennessee that day. Withering Federal artillery and musketry,
augmented by a few thousand repeating rifles, piled up
Confederate corpses in the ditches before the earthworks. Near the
right center of the line, there was a momentary breakthrough, but
Federal reserve forces pugged the whole. Constant fire killed many
Confederates as they hugged the ground, keeping them from
withdrawing after the initial attacks had failed. Even the setting of
the sun brought no end to the carnage; Hood sent in a fresh
division, lighting the way with torches, only to have these men
slaughtered as well. Early the next morning, Schofield pulled
away, having suffered only 2,300 casualties to Hood's 7,000. Six
of Hood's generals, including the brave and skillful Cleburne, had
been killed, and dozens of regimental commanders had been lost.
As one veteran later wrote, the Battle of Franklin became the
graveyard of the Army of Tennessee.[14]

Compared to many Confederate regiments at Franklin, the
66th Georgia suffered slight losses: two officers and one private
wounded. The enlisted man, seventeen-year-old Thomas Weaver
of Company K, was one of six children of a lower-class Sumter
County farmer. Weaver's wound was not serious, and he returned
to the ranks shortly after the battle. Unfortunately, the same could
not be said for the regiment's acting commander, Lieutenant
Colonel Hamilton. A bullet pierced the right side of Hamilton's
head, cutting several nerves and leaving him permanently blind in

[13] Ibid., 180–84, 238–40.
[14] Ibid., 268–71.

one eye. Hamilton's army service was over. Major Hull was also severely wounded at Franklin.[15] With Hamilton and Hull disabled, early-war veteran Captain Moses Brown of Company E was left the ranking officer in the regiment, but only for a few days. Brown's foot wound from his Virginia service, suddenly abscessed, and his left leg became almost useless. In great pain, Brown resigned from field duty on 9 December and spent the rest of the war serving on a medical examination board. [16] The few surviving lieutenants of the 66th Georgia were now in charge of the remnant of their old regiment.

After pausing to bury its dead, the Army of Tennessee limped towards Nashville. Unable to storm the strong Federal earthworks, and unwilling to concede defeat and withdraw, Hood erected a short, entrenched line south of the city. He had less than 20,000 men left, against Thomas's 60,000, and his supplies had all but withered. Against desperate, practically hopeless odds, Hood held on. To force Thomas to attack his fortified line and give him the advantage, Hood tried to capture isolated Federal outposts. In particular, Hood hoped to take Murfreesboro, southwest of Nashville, or at least threaten the town and induce Thomas to come out and fight.[17]

Bate's Division, augmented by some of Forrest's cavalry, was sent towards Fortress Rosecrans, a large Federal post at Murfreesboro. Tearing up the railroad to Nashville and constantly harassing Federal patrols and blockhouses, Bate provoked a strong response. On 7 December, part of the Federal garrison sallied forth from the fortress to attack him. Posted behind log barricades at the edge of a large field, Bate's men waited with rifles at the

[15] CSRs for Algernon S. Hamilton, Robert N. Hull, and Thomas H. Weaver; Eighth Census, 1860, Georgia, free inhabitants, Sumter County.
[16] Moses L. Brown CSR.
[17] Sword, *Embrace an Angry Wind,* 278–85.

ready. When the Yankees came into range, the Confederates tore into them. The Federal assault ground to a halt, and their lines threatened to come apart. Some of Forrest's men made ready to spring an ambush. For a moment, it seemed that a minor Confederate victory might be in the making, but then there were shouts of confusion from the center of Bate's line. Some of his men panicked and began running away. The disorder spread to the rest of the division, and within minutes the Confederates fell back, and the Federals returned to Fortress Rosecrans with prisoners and captured flags. Failing to rally Bate's fleeing men, the disgusted Forrest withdrew.[18]

What caused the sudden rout? One historian blames Jackson's Georgians for precipitating the panic by accidentally firing on a Florida brigade. Evidently, some of the Confederates were wearing blue uniforms taken from dead and wounded Yankees at Franklin, and Jackson's men mistook them for the enemy. Bate himself blamed the Georgians for the debacle at Second Murfreesboro.[19] Jackson denied that his men had caused the panic. Rather, Bate had made an error that forfeited the victory. "I have no doubt what-so-ever," Jackson bitterly told General Cheatham, "[that] the enemy would have been signally routed," had not Bate repeatedly moved the brigade around trying to plug holes in his line. This constant shuffling of the Georgians threw the entire division into disarray, and when they finally got into position, part of the line was already retreating and the day was lost.[20] Jackson's men, their commander claimed, had fought hard to save the division from

---

[18] Ibid., 293–99.

[19] Ibid., 297. I have chosen to call this engagement *Second* Murfreesboro in order to distinguish it from the first battle there in December 1862–January 1863.

[20] Henry R. Jackson to Benjamin F. Cheatham, 10 or 16 December 1864, *Confederate Reminiscences and Letters, 1861–1865*, vol. 3 (Georgia Division, United Daughters of the Confederacy, 1998) 193–96.

destruction, only to be slighted later when Bate implied that the Georgians had not been engaged. If that was true, Jackson argued, then the brigade's heavy casualties were proof of Bate's incompetent handling of the division.[21] Jackson may have been correct that most of his regiments suffered at Second Murfreesboro, but not in the case of the 66th Georgia. Once again, because of good fortune—or, perhaps, because they had not stayed around long enough—the regiment had passed through the battle almost unscathed. Only five men were counted as casualties.

One week after Bate's Division rejoined the Army of Tennessee, General Thomas finally emerged from Nashville and attacked Hood. The 66th Georgia, with the rest of Bate's men, sat out the first day of the battle on 15 December. Towards evening they were forced to withdraw when Federals outflanked Hood's left and it collapsed. Bate moved to the right center of a new line a few miles to the south. Short of food, clothing, and artillery ammunition, Hood's men waited for the next attack. It came late the following day. Hood had stretched his already-thin line even thinner. Bate's Division was forced to cover far too much ground with little more than 1,600 men. Seconds after the Federals assaulted Bate, his line began to unravel. As the Confederates fell back, Jackson was caught between Federal forces firing into his flank and rear and others assaulting his front. His Georgians broke and ran, and Jackson was captured when he slipped in the mud.[22] All along Hood's line, the rest of the Confederates peeled away in flight, abandoning guns, cannon, and baggage. It was Missionary Ridge all over again. A small rearguard kept Thomas's men from completely destroying the Army of Tennessee, but the losses were bad enough. Almost 7,000 Confederates became casualties at

---

[21] Ibid.
[22] Ibid., 370–76.

Nashville.[23] To this number the 66th Georgia contributed a little more than two dozen: three dead, two wounded, and twenty-two captured.

Defeat at Nashville had been catastrophic for the Army of Tennessee; the retreat that followed was calamitous. In a cold, stinging rain, the Confederates staggered south, hounded by the enemy cavalry. Time and again, Hood's men had to stop and fight rear-guard actions to hold off Thomas's pursuit. In one of these fights, on 17 December near Franklin, the 66th Georgia lost one man wounded and ten men captured, a greater loss than the regiment had suffered there on 30 November. Discipline almost completely broke down along the way, and rather than keep freezing, going hungry, and risking death, many Confederates surrendered or deserted. Perhaps 15,000 managed to get back safely to Alabama.[24]

Once the campaign ended, tongues began wagging about who was responsible for the outcome. The army's commander received the lion's share of the blame, and Hood soon resigned his command. As often happened in the Army of Tennessee, various commanders and units also targeted their comrades. Some in the army blamed Bate's Division, and particularly Jackson's Brigade, for the defeats at Franklin and Nashville. Incensed by the criticism, one member of Jackson's brigade, under the nom de plume "Officer," penned a rebuttal. He claimed that Bate had personally approved of their conduct during the campaign, that Bate "loved them like brothers," and that Bate, retracting his earlier criticisms, had said Jackson's Georgians kept cool when other units were "panic-stricken." Proof of the brigade's good fighting record could be found in the casualty lists, for "out of nine hundred men who crossed the Tennessee River, General

---

[23] Ibid., 425.
[24] Ibid., 392–422, 426.

Jackson lost three hundred and fifty, killed and wounded, and three hundred captured." Those who found fault with the Georgians, "Officer asserted, were "stay-at-homes" who ought to shoulder a musket themselves before they dared to criticize braver men.[25]

Many of Jackson's men were too tired, disillusioned and depressed to be so affronted. They had been through an unmitigated disaster, their army had been shattered, and the days of the Confederacy were numbered. For James Harrell of the 66th Georgia, the writing was on the wall; why fight any longer for a lost cause? Sometime in early 1865, Private Harrell stole away from Company C and tramped north to Nashville. There, on 19 January, Harrell raised his right hand before a United States Army officer and swore allegiance to the nation he had fought against for two years. Harrell was the last known deserter from the 66th Georgia.[26]

A total of fifty-three men from the regiment joined the Union Army during the war. Of that number, 11 (roughly 20 percent) claimed either to have been conscripted or to have enlisted in order to avoid conscription.

A couple of disparate references suggest that a significant percentage of the men in the 66th Georgia were compelled to serve. P. D. Stephenson, an artillerist in Bate's Division, described Jackson's Brigade as "Georgia conscripts almost entirely, poor material at best and the 'butt' of the rest of us." As most regiments in the brigade were actually volunteer units formed early in the war, before conscription, these remarks might refer to the 66th.

---

[25] *Macon Daily Telegraph,* 11 February 1865.
[26] James Harrell CSR.

Also, a requisition for fuel in summer 1863, signed by Captain Hull, classifies the regiment as "Conscripts."[27]

However, these references are not beyond challenge. Stephenson's remark is suspect, as that it was made after the war, when early-war veterans mythologized their services, minimized their own shortcomings, criticized late-war soldiers such as those of the 66th Georgia. As for the requisition, Confederate units formed after April 1862 were often classified as "conscript" regiments, even when most of their men were volunteers. And, if many of Nisbet's men entered the army against their will, why did so few of those who switched sides describe themselves as conscripts?

It is hardly possible to arrive at an answer by looking at the conscripts' demographics. Five of the alleged turncoats—Henry Beasley, Solomon Bedingfield, James Miller, Henry Stevens, and John Thomas—appear in the census records. They had little common ground between them. There is one teenager in the group, one man in his twenties, one in his thirties, and two who were at least forty years old. Beasley, Stevens, and Thomas were penniless, but Bedingfield and Miller owned at least $2,500 in property each, though the two had a combined total of eight children to support. Beasley and Stevens came from North Georgia, where both anti-Confederate and anti-war sentiments could be quite strong. Bedingfield, Miller, and Thomas hailed from south-central Georgia, an area that largely supported the Confederacy. [28] Thus neither the ages of these men, their means,

---

[27] *The Civil War Memoirs of P. D. Stephenson,* ed. Nathan Hughes (Conway: University of Central Arkansas Press, 1995) 300; unfiled item, Robert N. Hull CSR.

[28] See CSRs for Henry Beasley, Solomon E. Bedingfield, James A. Miller, Henry C. Stephens, and John H. Thomas. In his sample of later-enlisting Confederates, Noe found that "what can be said about the few conscripts studied…is that economically they ran across the spectrum" (*Reluctant Rebels,* 108–109).

nor the locations of their homes explain why they switched sides. None of these men left during the 1863–1864 winter encampment at Dalton, when most of Georgia's turncoat soldiers went over to the Union. [29] All were captured by the Union army during the Atlanta Campaign or in Alabama in late 1864. Maybe they identified as conscripts in order to escape Northern prisoner-of-war camps and serve on the western frontier. A few specifically mentioned the Amnesty Proclamation, which would allow them to take an oath of allegiance and return home. Once they were back in the South, what was to stop them from rejoining the Confederate Army?[30] In summary, these supposed conscripts might have been disingenuous to their captors.

The other turncoats defy easy categorization. Their ages ran the gamut, from nineteen-year-old farmhand John Beaver to forty-five-year-old farmer William Hudgens. Nine of the nineteen were penniless, and another nine owned less than $700 in property. Two-thirds came from the hotbeds of dissent, upcountry Georgia and the Upper Piedmont. Complicating the picture, more than half of the turncoats were prisoners captured during the Chattanooga, Atlanta, and Tennessee campaigns.[31] Although the demographics suggest a class- and location-based hostility to the Confederacy, we cannot be certain whether most were principled dissenters, or whether, upon finding themselves suddenly facing Federal muskets, they tried to convince their enemies that they had never wanted to fight in the first place.

---

[29] Weitz, "A Higher Duty," 118–19.

[30] In response to such abuses, Union army officials finally made a distinction between Confederate deserters, who were thought to be genuine conscripts, and Confederate prisoners, who were not to be trusted (ibid., 61–62).

[31] Including both men found in the sample and those who were not, thirty-three of the fifty-three men who switched sides did so after they were captured.

We should also wonder what made the remaining men of the 66th Georgia keep fighting after retreating from Tennessee. Alongside the "die-hards" who hated the Yankees and ached to avenge defeat would have been staunch optimists who expected ultimate victory at some point in the future. The greater part had probbaly yielded to peer pressure, pride, and loyalty to comrades, even if they had personally lost faith in the Confederate cause. One private named Clinton believed that the army contained more genuine Confederates than the home front. "The people of [Georgia] darling…would go back [to the Union] just to save their property," Clinton wrote his wife in January, "but I am truly glad to find the Soldiers so hopeful. Most of them say fight to the last."[32]

It was with men like Clinton, few in number but determined to win—or simply too ashamed to desert—-that the 66th Georgia fought its last campaign. With the other remnants of the Army of Tennessee, the regiment was sent to South Carolina in early 1865. Traveling along rickety railroads through burned-over Central Georgia, home to many of the men, the 66th reached its destination without any known desertions. In South Carolina, the regiment became part of about 30,000 Confederates trying to stop Sherman from marching to join Federal forces besieging Lee at Petersburg, Virginia. General Johnston was once again in command, to the delight of many, but Johnston could do no more than delay Sherman, who outnumbered him by more than three to one.

---

[32] Clinton to wife, 21 January 1865, Crane letters, AHC. Though Clinton's last name is not given, and no soldier of that first name can be found in the muster roll, the contents of his letters suggest that he was a member of the regiment.

One delaying action in South Carolina cost the 66th Georgia dearly. In late January, Sherman's army approached Columbia, the state capital. Only the 66th and a few other Confederate units were on hand to oppose him at Binnaker's Bridge, which crossed the Edisto River southwest of the city, and they were not in a good state. As Federal pickets approached on 8 February, Major Hull, who had recovered from his wound at Franklin, dashed off a quick note to his brother-in-law. "My men are completely demoralized," Hull confessed, "and I fear when the crisis comes they will be found wanting. Nevertheless, I shall do my duty."[33] Hull had been through numerous battles, but this one felt different; "a presentiment of evil" overshadowed him and he did not expect "to see another sun set." He would not. The following day, Lieutenant Colonel J. C. Gordon, commander of the consolidated 1st/66th, reported that the bridge had been taken and that "Major Hull...was killed."[34] For the third time, the 66th Georgia had lost its commanding officer, as well as a lieutenant (James Conner of Company A) and five enlisted men.[35]

Facing little opposition, Sherman's men captured Columbia and bridged numerous swamps and rivers as they marched through South Carolina, destroying public and private property. In North Carolina, Johnston waited for a chance to strike at the divided Federal columns. Finally, at Bentonville (19–21 March 1865), he cut into Sherman's left with a surprise attack that made some headway before being halted. It was all in vain; Sherman

---

[33] Robert N. Hull to brother-in-law, 8 February 1865, cited at "Elizabeth Maxey Berrie Hull Tucker," www.woodenshipsironmen.com/Articles/Berry.htm

[34] Ibid.; US War Department, *The War of the Rebellion: A Compilation of the Official Records of the Union and Confederate Armies* (Washington, DC: US Government Printing Office, 1880–1901) vol. 47, pt. 2, pp. 1134–35 (Hereafter cited as *OR*; all citations are from series 1 unless otherwise noted.).

[35] James A. Conner CSR.

brought up the rest of his army, counter-attacked, and drove Johnston from the field. Though the 66th Georgia lost a mere nine men at Bentonville, one of these casualties was the last voice from the ranks of the regiment, Sergeant James Crane, forever silenced. About a month after the battle, an Athens newspaper printed Sergeant Crane's obituary. He was described as a valiant soldier and—despite the scant piety of his letters—a good Christian:

> His military career was noble... He was twice wounded slightly, but never rested in consequence, as many might do... His captain writes of him that *"he was the best boy in his company."* He was...faithful in the discharge of the duties of prayer and Bible reading... [In the army] he made a covenant with one of his comrades to abstain from the vices of the soldier.... His honored parents...have the consolation that he is translated from the toils of sufferings of this life, to the joys and glories of the live to come... His remains rest upon the battlefield.[36]

The same day Crane's obituary appeared, his old army laid down its arms. Johnston, having learned that Lee's army had abandoned Petersburg and Richmond on 2 April and surrendered to Grant's encircling army at Appomattox Courthouse on 9 April, decided that further resistance was hopeless. He asked Sherman for a cease-fire, and two weeks later, Johnston's forces stacked their weapons at Durham Station, northwest of Raleigh.

At the time of the surrender, the 66th Georgia had undergone another reorganization, serving the last few weeks of the war as part of the 1st Georgia Confederate Battalion, which included the remnants of four other regiments.[37] Another sizeable part of the regiment, either deserters or those left behind from lack of

---

[36] *Athens Southern Watchman*, 26 April 1865.
[37] *OR*, vol. 47, pt. 1, p. 1065.

transportation, surrendered to Federal forces at Macon in early May. Forty-one men in North Carolina and 92 in Georgia were all that remained of the 1,021 who had marched off in summer 1863.

Who were those that remained until the end? Let their demographics tell the story. Two captains, one lieutenant, eight sergeants, one corporal, an assistant quartermaster, a commissary sergeant, regimental color-bearer J. D. McCay, and 118 privates were paroled at Durham Station and Macon. Captains J. D. Hunter and William Weaver were the senior officers present at the surrenders. Six of the surrendered men were early-war veterans, but only one, Captain Weaver, held an officer's commission.

Fifty-one of the men who surrendered appear in the census reports. They represent every region of Georgia, though a clear majority come from the Plantation Belt, especially Newton County. Half were younger than age thirty, including the regiment's youngest known soldier, teenaged Sergeant Dailey. Twenty-one were thirty-five or older, and the oldest in the group was planter John Chance (fifty-three). Thirty-six were farmers or from farming backgrounds. Twenty men were married fathers, among them J. H. Langford, who, unlike so many others in the regiment, could go back home to his twelve children.

The two richest men in the group of surrendering soldiers were slave owners. J. M. White of Company C and Joseph Eley of Company G owned $16,000 and $12,800 in assets, respectively.[38] Most of this wealth was in human property, now, of course, lost. Twenty-nine others had no property and another eight owned less than $500. Some—such as Captain Weaver, Sergeant Calvin Till, Quartermaster Sergeant Ascon Moody, and Privates Jasper Chapin, William Kimbrough, and Charles Lane—came from

---

[38] See appendices B and C; also, Eighth Census, 1860, Georgia, free inhabitants, Newton County.

well-to-do families. Though uncertain, their futures would probably be brighter than those of Ivey Allen and Arthur Williams, both penniless farmers and both responsible for taking care of several children.[39] Having risked all, Allen and Williams likely lost what little they had before the war. The same might have been true for the eighty-two surrendered men who were not found in the census records.

Those of the 66th Georgia who remained to surrender were not simply impoverished men with no other options. Some men of moderate to considerable means who had not bought their way out of service. For reasons known only to themselves, 133 soldiers of the 66th Georgia, from backgrounds both rich and poor, held out until spring 1865, long after many others, some far wealthier and some just as destitute, had called it quits. All of the regiment's veterans would have to start all over again in a ruined land.

Spring 1865 found James Cooper Nisbet standing at the gate of Cloverdale. He barely recognized his old stock farm; fences had been torn down, equipment had been destroyed, and all of the livestock was gone. As most of the damage had been done during the Chattanooga Campaign, when Nisbet was nearby and visited, his surprise might not have been as great as he claimed. Regardless, it was time to rebuild: "I would sow wheat. With help if I could get it; without it, if nobody could be hired."[40]

That Nisbet had returned home was a miracle. After being captured at the Battle of Atlanta—and nearly bayoneted by one of his captors—hustled to the rear, and loaded into a box- car with hundreds of other Confederate prisoners, Nisbet had been sent to Johnson's Island, a prisoner-of-war camp on Lake Erie near

---

[39] Ibid.

[40] James C. Nisbet, *Four Years on the Firing Line* (Chattanooga TN: Imperial Press, 1911) 386–87.

Sandusky, Ohio. On the island, temperatures sometimes dropped below zero, firewood had to be rationed, and the prisoners, in their hunger, often ate rats. What most enraged Nisbet was the needless suffering he and his comrades endured on Johnson's Island. In retaliation for the scanty rations fed to Union prisoners, the prison authorities decreed that the Confederates would receive no more than an equal measure.[41] "Notwithstanding I had three hundred and fifty dollars to my credit," sent by relatives, Nisbet "was not allowed to purchase anything—for myself or friends— that would allay hunger." Attempts to smuggle in food led to seizure of the contraband items and restrictions on letter-writing privileges. Salted white-fish, salt pork and beef were all that kept the colonel and his fellow prisoners alive.[42] Cold, hungry, and with "one thin blanket to each man," the Confederates were treated harshly by their guards, men of the 128th Ohio Infantry. These Buckeyes, part of a home-guard unit, had no respect for real soldiers: "That we were Southerners," Nisbet remembered, "was enough for them!" If the Confederates failed to extinguish their candles at "lights out," the Ohioans would shoot into the windows, often killing or wounding the prisoners.[43]

When news arrived of the surrenders of Lee and Johnston, Nisbet hoped for a quick release, but for a time it seemed that his hopes might be dashed. Federal prisoners returning from Andersonville told horror stories about that camp, "enough lies," as Nisbet classified them, "to satisfy the Yankee craving for the Munchausen."[44] The assassination of President Lincoln just one

---

[41] Ibid., 313–63.

[42] Ibid.

[43] Ibid.

[44] Though Andersonville had one of the highest death rates of any prisoner-of-war camp—nearly 33 percent—and the privations of Union prisoners were real enough, Nisbet believed to the end of his life that Johnson's Island and

week after Appomattox had doubled Northern fury towards the south. An angry Congress was talking of charging all imprisoned Confederate officers with treason. Nisbet feared he might stay in prison forever, or be hanged "to satisfy the demand for more blood." Once tempers finally cooled, a policy of mercy prevailed, and Nisbet was released from Johnson's Island.[45]

The former Confederate colonel began his journey home in September 1865, returning by way of New York to stay with "friends of my father [who] received me cordially." Traveling down the Eastern seaboard, Nisbet passed through the Carolinas, visiting the ruins of Columbia and other places where his regiment had fought. At long last, Nisbet reached Georgia and was reunited with his father, mother, and brother John; "there was a happy family reunion...the two boys restored to the family, sound, well, after passing through many battles." The Confederacy had fallen, but "we were all very happy."[46]

With Georgia in shambles and money short, Nisbet had to find some work. He journeyed to Macon and discovered "warehouses full of cotton" going to waste because the state's wrecked railroads could not ship to buyers. There were, however, a surplus of ex-army mules on hand. Nisbet saw the solution clearly: he would buy the mules, sell them to cotton brokers, and then use the profits to fix up Cloverdale. Forming a partnership with his brother-in-law, Nisbet entered the draying business with a vengeance; "'quick sales and small profits' was my motto." For the best mules, Nisbet received over $400, and "as the times got settled,...I had cleared four good mules to take to my farm, and

---

other Northern camps were just as lethal for Confederate prisoners (ibid., 334–36).

[45] Nisbet, *Four Years,* 359–63.

[46] Ibid., 363–69.

money enough to rebuild considerable fencing and sow a small…crop."[47]

During his time in Macon, Nisbet ran into a few veterans of the 66th Georgia, including Charles Williamson and Briggs Napier. Whenever they met, the talk inevitably turned to those who had died. "We missed many of our boyhood friends," Nisbet confessed. Even as he spoke, many more were passing away. Worn down and in broken health, some of Nisbet's men did not survive the war by long. Thomas Perry, a private in Company I who had been captured during the retreat from Nashville, developed an infection from an earlier wound at Franklin. Just two months after Johnston's surrender, he passed away. James Conner of Company A, wounded at Atlanta and again at Binnaker's Bridge, died sometime in 1865. War wounds sent Daniel O'Rear to his grave in 1869. John Chance of Company B contracted bronchitis in his last few weeks of service and succumbed in 1870.[48]

Some of Nisbet's veterans might well have wished for the mercy of an early grave. For Lorenzo Belisle, the end of the war was followed by a quarter-century of misery. The second bullet that hit Belisle at Peach Tree Creek had destroyed one of his testicles, severely damaged his penis, and shredded the muscles of his inner thigh. Belisle did not die from what ought to have been a fatal wound, but he was never again the same man. He suffered from constant urethral bleeding and had great difficulty urinating. He could not work, he could hardly move, and heart problems from an early-war sickness often left him barely able to breathe.[49]

"[Capt. Belisle] appeared to be a great sufferer," reported a boardinghouse matron who took care of him. "[There] was

---

[47] Ibid., 370–74.

[48] Ibid., 375–76; CSRs for Thomas R. Perry, James Conner, Daniel O'Rear, and John T. Chance.

[49] Belisle pension application, GCPA.

something the matter with his throat...and [he] had to eat with great care, to keep from getting choked [sic]." Because of his wounds, Belisle "slept with his head and shoulders propped up till he was about a half sitting posture." In that position, Belisle's breathing difficulties increased, and at times the matron had to shake him awake if he "seemed...helpless and was...making a noise as though he was choking." Beset with spells of temporary paralysis, the old Confederate got through each night as best he could, battling the terrors of what he had seen and the fear that he might not wake up. "He...never allowed the light turned out in his room while he slept," the matron recalled, "and I have often known him to stay awake until after mid night...he felt, if he went to sleep he would be troubled."[50]

Belisle found some monetary relief from state-issued yearly pensions, but he also encountered bureaucratic callousness. When a friend who delivered his application one year arrived slightly late at the pension office, Belisle complained, "the Commissioner simply pigeon-holed my papers and told my friend that it aught be next fall before he examined them." "God help me," Belisle asked woefully, "was my 4 years service and suffering...for 35 years not worth 30 minutes of a state official's time[?]." Determined to get the money he needed, Belisle submitted a lengthy application in 1889. The full package numbered twenty-nine pages and "measured seven and a half feet in length," and included several doctor's letters testifying to his incapacity. "I have not been able to cut...firewood in twelve years," Belisle told the governor. "I have not been able to walk a mile...[and] I can't raise no weight with [my] left hand." There was little that could be done for the captain; even his pension, a newspaper noted, was "totally inadequate to his sufferings."[51]

---

[50] Ibid.
[51] Ibid; *Atlanta Constitution*, 9 August 1889.

Other veterans, of sound bodies but worried minds, seemed listless. "Many...who had returned from the army," Nisbet remembered sadly, "were to be seen...playing billiards and sitting around, damning their luck...and telling war yarns, between drinks."[52] Their melancholy owed to great difficulties in paying bills and putting food on the table. The devastation wrought the war, especially in the Plantation Belt, left many veterans destitute.

To ease their sufferings, at least 180 of Nisbet's veterans or their widows followed Belisle's example and applied for Confederate pensions. Poverty was the necessary condition for application, and the meager payments—about $50 for incapacitated veterans or $100 for widows—were not likely to change it. Applicants were asked to estimate their earnings from previous years; how much property they owned, and its value; how much they needed in support, and how much of this they could contribute. In a few cases, such as that of William Inglett, applicants claimed they could cover one-quarter to one-half of their support themselves.[53] The overwhelming majority of applications, however, included the same few words that spoke of the hardships wrought by a destructive war, "Can contribute nothing."

Forty-five pension applicants or applicants' husbands can be found in the census records. A little less than half of them had been poor men owning nothing before the war. Nine had owned less than $500 worth of property. Larger fortunes, too, had been laid waste. George Murrah, whose prewar assets had totaled $2,575, now made about $50 a year. Graves Weaver, the regiment's commissary sergeant, had lost most of his $4,425; since then, his children had supported him. Adam Williamson of Company I, a possible deserter during the Atlanta Campaign,

---

[52] Nisbet, *Four Years*, 373.
[53] W. J. L. Inglett, 1897, GCPA, Columbia County.

begged for $60 in support, his $4,900 in real and personal property gone to ashes. Even the widow of Captain Charles Williamson (no relation), one of the wealthier men in the officer corps of the 66th, had little left to live on after the family's house and lot, worth about $3,500, were sold and divided between her and the children.[54]

Hardly any applicants owned land. The few that did frequently described their holdings as worthless. John Gentry held title to 50 acres in Gordon County, which if sold could, he estimated, fetch about a dollar an acre. Widow Rebecca St. Johns was much better off; her 2 1/2 acres were worth about $200. Another widow, Sarah Stephens, had 32 acres, worth $500. Bad harvests, creditors, or dead or injured husbands left most of the applicants in the same situation as Marie Maddox and S. E. Taylor; both widows had been forced to part with their lands, valued at $600 and $1,000, respectively, to pay off debts.[55] Forced emancipation had also affected some of Nisbet's men. Fifteen former slave owners or sons of slave-owning families applied for the pensions. Among their number was John Wilkes of Company A. Once he had held the power of life and death over, and controlled the productive means of, at least 50 human beings. With slavery destroyed, Wilkes asked for help just to get by.[56]

---

[54] J. J. Dixon pension application, 1906, ibid., Madison County; George W. Murrah pension application, 1912, ibid., Richmond County; Adam A. Williamson pension application, 1898, ibid., Jackson County; Charles J. Williamson pension application, 1910, ibid., Bibb County.

[55] J. P. Gentry pension application, 1899, ibid., Gordon County; R. J. St. Johns pension application, 1912, ibid., Morgan County; Sarah H. Stephens pension application, 1912, ibid., Walton County; Marie F. Maddox pension application, 1910, ibid., Troup County; S. E. Taylor pension application, 1892, ibid., Clark County.

[56] John A. Wilkes pension application, 1895, ibid., Jackson County.

There was little better in store for most of these men. The economic renewal of the "New South," which turned the smoking ruins of Atlanta into a bustling metropolis, was an urban phenomenon that barely touched their lives. Instead, sharecropping and tenancy would trap the majority of them on unfruitful plots, worked to death by unsympathetic owners. They would spend day after day in hard toil with little to show for it; would hear of great fortunes made in cotton but barely earn pennies themselves; and (some of them, certainly) would have wondered what benefits, if any, had been made in their lives from two years of deadly, thankless service.

Physical, fiscal, and emotional troubles then, loomed large for Nisbet's veterans, but they did their best to persevere. There were long-delayed marriages to enter into, such as that of Briggs Napier and Bessie Reed; children to raise, including one daughter born to the badly crippled Lorenzo Belisle; families to take care of, a duty for the recovered John Davis; and lives to live, however challenging. On occasion, too, there were tangible successes to celebrate. A handful of Nisbet's men entered politics, and it should come as no surprise that Nisbet himself was the most prominent. He represented Dade County in the Georgia Assembly from 1868 to 1870, and was championed for opposing what one paper called the "invasions of radicalism and the plunderers and corruptionists" of Reconstruction, under the Republican Governor Rufus Bullock. Nisbet followed his legislative service with a position as general secretary of the Georgia Constitutional Convention of 1877.[57] Algernon Hamilton, blind in one eye from Franklin, also entered the legislature and served at the 1877 Constitutional Convention. Other veterans became civic boosters.

---

[57] Corbin, "Reminiscences of Briggs Hopson Napier"; Belisle pension application, GCPA; Nisbet, *Four Years*, 373, 395–405; *Atlanta Weekly Constitution*, 17 July 1877.

Thomas Langston and Cecil Hammock, once captain and assistant quartermaster of the regiment respectively, moved to Atlanta and became involved in developing the city, Langston as a grocer and Hammock as a real estate agent and alderman.[58] These few who made their mark in the public world were exceptional; most veterans of the 66th simply picked up where they had left off on large and small farms and in skilled and unskilled jobs.

In their final years, Confederate veterans began gathering to remember old times, tell and retell war stories, venerate the leaders of the Confederacy, and simply enjoy each other's company. The 66th Georgia joined the 1st Georgia Confederate Infantry for a joint reunion in summer 1895 on the Chickamauga battlefield, even though the 66th had not fought there. A program for the reunion, printed in the *Macon Telegraph,* shows a fairly typical order of events. After invocational music and a prayer by Reverend T. R. Hardin, the soldiers sang a wartime favorite, "Tenting Tonight on the Old Campground." A brief welcome by newspaper editor W. Troy Bankston was followed by a rendition of "Dixie," then an address by John H. Reece, former captain of the 1st Georgia Confederate Infantry, a singing of the anthem "America," and a roll call of survivors. There was an honoring of the dead, a parting song, "God Be with You till We Meet Again," a barbecue dinner, and finally a benediction. As far as it appears, this was the only reunion of Nisbet's men. Veterans like Elias Eargle of Company K, removed to Texas, who wanted to reconnect with their comrades, had to do so through *Confederate Veteran* and other special publications.[59]

---

[58] *Brief Biographies of the Members of the Constitutional Convention, July 11, 1877; Atlanta Weekly Sun,* 18 January 1871; *Atlanta Georgian and News,* 9 January 1911.

[59] *Macon Telegraph,* 17 August 1895; *Confederate Veteran* 21/2 (February 1913): 92.

Just as Nisbet was the most notable of the regiment's veterans, so too was his memoir the only published account of the 66th Georgia. *Four Years on the Firing Line* (1911), 445 pages in length, appeared during Nisbet's seventy-third year. Most of what Nisbet wrote came from his own memories, though he also selectively sampled the *Official Records of the War of the Rebellion,* a voluminous compendium of wartime reports. Primarily a military history, *Four Years* occasionally delved into social and political issues from the antebellum and postwar eras. Nisbet denounced New England abolitionists as sanctimonious, meddling hypocrites, condemned prewar anti-slavery fighter John Brown as a blood-thirsty madman, and growled that the early twentieth-century United States had "a Government of the trusts, by the trusts and for the trusts!"[60]

Four Years marched in lockstep with the "Lost Cause" view of the Civil War. Confederate soldiers, described by Nisbet as invariably poor, fought not for slavery but for states' rights. Slavery was the "irritating" cause of the war, only because abolitionists had used it to drive a wedge between the two sections of the country and to deny the South her "rights." "The Southerner," Nisbet wrote, "was honest in his interpretation of the Constitution[, and] the North is beginning to view the situation in that same light." Reconstruction had been rank military despotism, Nisbet thundered, victimizing white Southerners and elevating African-American freedmen beyond their abilities. Thinking back to the slaves he had known in his youth, Nisbet pronounced all talk of equal rights for freedmen as foolish. "I have studied the full-blooded negro," he claimed, "[and] find it

---

[60] Nisbet, *Four Years,* 17–28, 420–24, 443.

impossible to disagree with the...conclusion that he is an inferior species of the human race."[61]

In one particular area did Nisbet differ from many of his contemporaries. He believed that the Confederacy lost the war not because of the North's greater numbers and resources, but because of the errors of its own leaders. Jefferson Davis in particular was the scapegoat for Appomattox. "The Southern soldier," Nisbet declared, *"would have succeeded, had he not been mismanaged!"* (emphases original).[62] Even in this regard, Nisbet displayed a bit of Virginia-centrism. His closing remarks in *Four Years* were of Gettysburg—a battle that in Nisbet's eyes underscored the mismanagement behind Confederate military disasters. "The...question settled there," he concluded, "was one of the ability of the [Northern army], on those rugged cliffs...to defeat [Lee's army, which had to march] through open plains, and under the fierce fire of musketry and cannon!"[63] Not even Hood's blunders around Atlanta made as good a case to Nisbet.

Nisbet spent more than half of his memoirs tracing ancestral connections and discussing the campaigns of the 21st Georgia. Though Nisbet was one of a very small group of junior officers who commanded men in both the Eastern and Western theaters, his memories of the former were more fleshed out. Nisbet greatly admired Robert E. Lee and Stonewall Jackson, and spent many pages on Confederate victories in Virginia. When he came to his service in the Western Theater, Nisbet resorted to acidic criticisms of Braxton Bragg and John Bell Hood, commendations of Joseph Johnston, and a few anecdotes about the 66th Georgia. As disappointing as it may be that Nibset's account of regimental

---

[61] Ibid., 17–28, 26–32, 66–76, 396–405, 409–439 (first quotation, 438–439, second quotation, 418).

[62] Nisbet, *Four Years*, 441.

[63] Ibid., 441–442, 444.

command is brief and perfunctory, compared to his memories of being a captain in Virginia, this is typical of Confederate reminiscences.[64]

Consigned to a peripheral sphere in the memoirs of its colonel, the 66th Georgia was also conspicuously absent in the publications of the Southern Historical Society, which articulated and shaped Southerners' view of the war. The closest thing to official recognition that Nisbet's men received were addresses that honored the army in which it served. At an 1880 meeting of the Army of Tennessee Association, Dr. Thomas Markham, who served as a chaplain in the army, applauded the long-suffering spirit of men like those of the 66th:

> When men march from victory to victory...then it is easy to be a soldier, then courage communicates and bravery becomes contagious. But to...fall back from point in toilsome marches...and then repulsed, yes, routed, to return pursued along roads just passed over as pursuers, this tests men, and all this tested these men, and they stood the test.... And...suffer me to say to you who here represent the glorious Virginia army.... Your defeats were fewer than our victories, and yet we do not ask you to be generous, but simply just, in yielding your assent, when we say that the men of the armies of the west...were your peers in spirit, in courage, and in devotion, and that tried (as you were not) by accumulation of disaster...they exceeded to the last, with a spirit that rose above reverses...illustrating that law laid down..."that human virtue should be equal to human calamity."[65]

---

[64] See Richard McMurry, *Two Great Rebel Armies: An Essay in Confederate Military History* (Chapel Hill: University of North Carolina Press, 1988) especially 5–9, for how the "Lee Tradition" of the late nineteenth century established the dominance of the eastern theater in Southern postwar memory.

[65] "A Tribute to the Army of Tennessee," *Southern Historical Society Papers* 8/8–9 (August and September 1880): 511–15.

At another meeting of the association in 1883, Colonel William Preston Johnston, son of slain Confederate General Albert Sidney Johnston, paid tribute to the often-defeated Western army. "We did our duty," Preston Johnston told his aging comrades, "and whether victory crowned our arms, or the inextinguishable fires of hate…pour upon us the consequences of defeat, yet it is well with us." Preston Johnston described the Army of Tennessee as the Confederacy's shield, which "bore all of the tests of as high a resolution, and of as noble endurance" as the Army of Northern Virginia, the Confederacy's "sword."[66]

There was nothing specific to the 66th in what Preston Johnston or Markham said, but their overarching tributes would have to do. Far more surprising was the exclusion of the regiment and its officers from an article about Walker's Division that appeared in the *Macon Weekly Telegraph* in 1867. Theodore Winn, a veteran of the 25th Georgia, omitted the 66th from the organization of Wilson's Brigade, which according to Winn consisted of his own regiment plus "the 29th and 30th Georgia regiments, 4th Louisiana battalion and 1st battalion Georgia sharpshooters." Nearly every regimental commander in the brigade was a great man, according to Winn, but no mention was made of Nisbet, who had more combat experience than any of the others and who had once commanded the brigade. It seems hard to escape the conclusion that, in Winn's mind, the 66th Georgia was never really a part of Wilson's Brigade, either because it was a late-war regiment, because it included conscripts, or because it had missed the battle at Chickamauga.

Some of Nisbet's men must have read and taken offense to the article, yet none of them countered it in veterans' publications such as *Confederate Veteran* and *Southern Bivouac*. Though they

---

[66] "The Army of Tennessee," *Southern Historical Society Papers* 11/1 (January 1883): 40–43.

remained silent, their families sometimes did not. A few women related to the veterans of the 66th offered their own memories to the *Veteran* and to local chapters of the United Daughters of the Confederacy (UDC). These women offered a nostalgic, Lost-Cause-tinged look at the families who supported the 66th.

Kathryn Bradford shared a story of how her great grand-mother, Rebecca, left six children at home in Putnam County in summer 1864 to retrieve a sick husband, Lewis Rossee of Company F. While Rebecca was absent, a Union patrol swarmed over the farm, "demanding all the food we had." One of the family's slaves, "Aunt Bessie," refused to help the soldiers and, when ordered to turn over the key to the smokehouse, "took that key out of her pocket and swallowed it." The angered Federals shot the lock off and took all the meat, leaving the Rossee children hungry. When their mother's wagon returned, they could see it was carrying a coffin; Lewis Rossee was dead from typhoid. "It's all right," Bradford's grandfather comforted Kathryn, "We know where Papa's buried."[67]

Eudora Weaver Stephenson, the daughter of Graves Weaver, titled her reminiscences "Refugeeing in War Time." Set in the later stages of the Atlanta Campaign, Eudora's story followed the fortunes of Weaver's family, who "tarried in an effort to harvest as much of the crop as possible" on their Gwinnett County farm. Hearing that Atlanta had fallen, the family left for an uncle's neighboring farm, but could not escape marauding Federal soldiers. Five hundred Yankees, according to Eudora, fell upon the farm, killed a Confederate cavalry scout who had camped there, chased off seven others, and then entered the farmhouse "breaking locks, searching every possible hiding place, principally for men and guns, but took jewelry, watches and anything else they

---

[67] *Confederate Reminiscences,* 11:150–51.

wanted."[68] Eudora's brother John hid a prized horse, but this was small recompense for the damage visited on the family's farm by another party of raiders: "The Yankees took down window curtains to smoke out the bees, and took all the honey.... The fowls were convenient for them, too.... They also took the horses...set fire to the houses and left." Sifting through the ruins, Eudora and her sister salvaged a loom and spun a new pair of trousers for their father before he left to rejoin the 66th in South Carolina. Carbuncles kept Weaver from working for some time after the war, but he had at least one silver dollar in his pocket when he returned home.[69]

By far, the most detailed tribute to a soldier of the 66th Georgia was penned by a young South Carolina girl, Annie Maria. Seven years after the skirmish at Binnaker's Bridge, Annie delivered "an appeal to the Ladies of Georgia" in the pages of the *Weekly Sumter Republican* on behalf of the slain Major Hull. "From where I am sitting now," she wrote, "I can see, under the shadow of the morning fires, a solitary grave—the last resting place of a brave young Georgian." Returning to 9 February 1865, Annie envisioned Sherman's soldiers passing by her home and, though she was very young at the time, "I remember the feeling of indignation and rebellion, that raged within me as I heard them talking in sneering tones of a 'fool of a rebel...who had tried to rally his men against them...and had been shot down in the act...and left...alone, wounded and dying.'"[70]

Annie's mother, too, burned with "a GENUINE REBEL FIRE," and demanded that the Federals bring "this brave defender of our rights...here to our house, that we may minister unto him." A sympathetic officer had Hull carried into the house; the

---

[68] *Confederate Veteran* 39/4 (April 1931): 136–38.
[69] Ibid.
[70] *Weekly Sumter Republican*, 1 November 1872.

Confederate had been badly wounded by a bullet that "had found its way to the brave, true, heart, and there alas! too well had it done its work of destruction." Hull rallied twice, crying out "Charge, men, charge!" in his delirium, then called for his mother, before "his sprit took its flight to join 'mother' in the realms above, or perhaps, there to await her coming."[71] Annie and her family buried Hull in his "jacket of gray" under an oak tree in the yard. Though the ceremony had been spare, Annie maintained that "no great general, buried with all the pomp and ceremony which the world knows how to accord…ever had truer, sincerer mourners than this brave young hero." Ever since, Annie and her friends had laid fresh flowers on the grave, anticipating that one day Hull's body would be sent home to his family. "Shall this one remain uncared for," she asked, "covered with pine straw and decaying leaves, and the name of him who sleeps here sink into oblivion?" Annie urged the Ladies Memorial Association of Atlanta to contact Hull's relatives, but nothing seems to have been done.[72] To this day, the mortal remains of Robert Newton Hull probably still lie near the Edisto River.

Hull's commander followed him to the grave more than half a century after Binnaker's Bridge. James Cooper Nisbet married twice, first to Mary E. Young of North Carolina in 1866, and then to Louise Bailey of Georgia. Four children—Mollie, Irene, Francis and Jones—were born to Nisbet, and he lived long enough to see Francis married in 1912. In 1902, Nisbet moved to Chattanooga and began writing letters to the Chickamauga-Chattanooga National Military Park insisting that, no matter what the official reports said, the 66th Georgia ought to have a monument on

---

[71] Ibid.
[72] Ibid.

Tunnel Hill. On 20 May 1917, Nisbet died and was buried in the Confederate Cemetery in Chattanooga.[73]

Many of Nisbet's old soldiers had gone before him. Others followed soon afterwards. Albert Jackson of Company C, returned from a Federal prisoner-of-war camp, had died in Newton County in 1918. Robert Sikes of Company I passed away in 1919. Charles Gray, a lieutenant in Company K—who had been wounded at Atlanta and Bentonville, represented Bibb County in the Georgia Assembly, and sponsored the bill that funded the Georgia state monument at Chickamauga—died in March 1920. Seven months later, John Parker, blind in his right eye from an exploding shell, passed away near Monroe. George Davis, wounded at Peach Tree Creek and left convalescing in Georgia during the Tennessee Campaign, died in 1921. W. F. McCart, Sr., one of those who served to the end and surrendered in North Carolina, died at the Confederate Soldiers Home in Atlanta in February 1923. Elias Eargle and W. H. Wilson both died in 1925; fellow privates John McGough and James Carrington followed them the next year; and Reuben Vann of Company D died in 1928. The last known survivor of the regiment was Ezekiel Askew. Twenty-four years old when he enlisted in Company G, Askew became sick during the Atlanta Campaign but survived, returned to his home in Greene County, and died there in 1935, having reached a venerable ninety-six years of age.[74]

---

[73] James C. Nisbet, *Four Years on the Firing Line,* rev. ed., ed. Belly I. Wiley (Chattanooga TN: Imperial Press, 1962) xvi–xvii; *Columbus Ledger,* 11 August 1912; 66th Georgia Unit File, Chickamauga-Chattanooga NMP Archives.

[74] CSRs for E. Griffin Askew, James T. Carrington, George W. Davis, Albert L. Jackson, W. F. McCart, Sr., John McGough, John William Parker, Reuben A. Vann, and W. H. Wilson; "Report of Deaths at Augusta, Georgia," www.confederatevets.com/documents; "Lieutenant Charles Gray," *Confederate Veteran* 28/11 (November 1920): 428; Eighth Census, 1860, Georgia, Free inhabitants, Greene County.

Four years after Askew died, the city that he and his regiment had fought for hosted the premiere of an iconic motion picture. *Gone With the Wind,* based on a 1936 novel about the Old South written by Atlanta native Margaret Mitchell, helped define the imagery and impact of the Civil War for generations to come. Among the visual treats of that film was an array of Confederate regalia in scenes of the Atlanta Campaign. Few who saw the film premiere could have known that the original model for many of these outfits was an old gray uniform, owned by film consultant Telamon C. S. Cuyler, that had once been worn by Cuyler's great-uncle, Lieutenant Colonel Algernon Hamilton.[75]

In a way, then, some of the essence of the 66th Georgia Infantry, and the men who served in its ranks, has been captured for all time. Though Cloverdale is gone, the battlefields of Atlanta are buried under concrete, and the Southern soldiers who signed up in 1863 have been consigned to cemeteries and fading letters, memory persists, filtered through drama. All but forgotten by fellow soldiers and historians, Nisbet and his band of conscripts, substitutes and volunteers march on, their legacy preserved, however vicariously, in one of the most popular visual tributes to the Confederate cause.

---

[75] "Telamon C. S. Cuyler," *History Notes* 3/1 (Spring 2005): 2.

Conclusion

Compared to other Civil War regiments, the record of the 66th Georgia Infantry seems unremarkable. It entered service when the war was halfway over, spent months in garrison duty and winter quarters, and did not experience a large battle until almost a year after being formed. When it finally fought, scant records make it difficult to ascertain exactly what happened to the regiment at Peach Tree Creek and Atlanta, and during the Tennessee Campaign. This study instead has looked at the quality and experience of the regiment's officers, the demographic composition of its ranks, and critiques of the postwar claims of its commander.

We return for one last look at the questions posed at the beginning of this book. What kinds of men served in the 66th Georgia? What were their backgrounds? Did they volunteer, or were they conscripted? How qualified were their officers? Did they serve faithfully, or did many desert? Finally, how well did the regiment fight, and what kept it going despite repeated defeats?

The sample taken for this study shows that the men of the 66th Georgia were mainly farmers or members of farming families. At least one-quarter were teenagers—somewhat younger than the typical Civil War soldier—and another quarter were in their mid-thirties to mid-forties and thus substantially older. Geographically, they came from all parts of the state, but the majority came from the Plantation Belt in south-central Georgia. Most were poor, owning no property and often belonging to families who owned nothing. A significant number must have been conscripts, although the majority were probably volunteers. At least 14 percent owned slaves or lived with slave-owning friends or families.

These findings contrast sharply with the demographics of early-war Confederate soldiers, who tended to be younger, middle class, and with a more significant connection to slavery. Whether the "boys of '61" were more motivated to fight and more imbued with Confederate patriotism than the "men of '63" is debatable. Certainly the earliest volunteers thought so; in their view, there was something wrong with fellow Southerners who had not joined the army immediately after Fort Sumter. Yet, "with a few exceptions later-enlisting men] proved to be willing soldiers, driven to defend their kin, homes, and property in an acceptably manly fashion not so unlike their [early-war] comrades."[1]

There is a difficulty in gauging how much Nisbet's officers shaped the 66th Georgia into "willing soldiers" ready to fight and die in an "acceptably manly fashion." Had they been entirely veteran, as Nisbet claimed, then the regiment might be an example of what prior combat experience could and could not provide in command ability. The truth, however, was that the vast majority of Nisbet's soldiers had never worn a uniform or witnessed a battle. How did this affect the selection of officers? Did the enlisted men of the 66th, who initially held the power to install or depose their lieutenants and captains, not value experience? Did they believe that the inexperienced men they chose had some intangible qualities of leadership that would eventually surface? Future studies of other late-war regiments may help to answer these questions.

One of the true tests of a combat unit is how it behaves when *not* under fire. Do the men desert or hold firm? As a whole, later-enlisting Confederate soldiers have been misunderstood ever since the end of the Civil War. They have been accused of cowardice

---

[1] Glatthaar, *General Lee's Army,* 18–21, 203–205; Kenneth W. Noe, *Reluctant Rebels: The Confederates who Joined the Army After 1861* (Chapel Hill: University of North Carolina Press, 2010) 195.

and are said to have avoided battle wherever possible. Usually it was early-war Confederates who made such accusations, and many historians have accepted their words as gospel truth.[2]

The statistics of attrition show that the 66th Georgia neither shirked battle nor suffered from an unusually large number of desertions. A total of 287 of Nisbet's men were killed, wounded, captured, or otherwise incapacitated by battle—almost one-quarter of the regiment's original strength. At least another 165 men died of or were incapacitated by sickness. Against these losses, eighty-six men were known to have deserted the regiment or went over to the Union.[3] This is less than one-third of the number killed, wounded, or captured, and about one-half of the number lost to sickness. Thus, a soldier in the 66th Georgia was five times more likely to succumb to a minie ball or a virus than to quit the regiment for home or a blue uniform. Altogether, the regiment lost one of every two men during the war from all causes combined.

In the first year of its service, the regiment did not suffer many losses in battle. The retreat from Dalton to Atlanta was not especially costly for Nisbet and his men. It was not until the battles for Atlanta, especially Peach Tree Creek, that the regiment suffered heavily, likely losing 70 percent of its effective strength in just a few weeks. These losses were doubly detrimental, because they included so many company officers as well as Colonel Nisbet. By contrast, the Tennessee and Carolina Campaigns resulted in comparatively light casualties for the 66th Georgia.

---

[2] Noe, *Reluctant Rebels,* 6–7, 198.

[3] This does not count men who deserted but returned, or the large number who disappeared from the muster rolls.

Table 3.
Attritional Losses of the 66th Georgia Infantry, All Causes

Cause of attrition	Number lost
Died, sickness	119
Wounded (not fatally)	109
Captured	96
Died as prisoners-of-war	43
Deserted	43
Switched sides	43
Died in or as a result of battle	37
Furloughed	18
Discharged	14
Disabled by sicknesss	14
Died, unknown causes	13
Resigned/retired	11
Died, at home	6
Transferred	5
Sworn out of service by habeas corpus	5
Missing	4
Detailed	4
Dropped from rolls	2
Disabled by wounds	2
Died, accident	1
Taken home by family	1
Total	589 (57% of total strength)

Desertion was not so serious a problem for the regiment. Most of those who deserted did so in summer and early fall 1863, while the companies were still filling out. The second largest number of desertions occurred during or in the aftermath of the Chattanooga Campaign. Desertion in the Atlanta Campaign was probably higher than the official records suggest, but no existing letters mention an extraordinarily high rate. Men were more likely to leave the regiment either during its formation or while it was inactive. In the first case, Camp Cooper in Macon was close enough to the regiment's principal home counties to encourage men to desert. With new recruits and draftees coming and going, it would have been easier for the disenchanted or unwilling to "slip out" then as opposed to later, once recruitment had ended, officers had been elected, and camp guards had been posted. In the second case, as with other regiments in the Army of Tennessee, the winter at Dalton probably produced a crisis of faith for some of Nisbet's men. As historian Mark Weitz has concluded, Georgia soldiers like those under Nisbet deserted in large numbers while they were encamped in North Georgia during winter 1864.[4] Once active campaigning began, desertions dramatically decreased. As to the demographics of deserters, while most were dirt-poor older men with large families to support, there were plenty of exceptions. Sometimes younger, single men or men with decent means left the service for good.

Table 4.
Losses from Combat, Chronologically, By Battle or Campaign[5]

Chattanooga Campaign (23–27 November 1863)	25
Atlanta Campaign (May–September, 1864)	
Resaca (9–15 May)	5
Dallas (25–27 May)	2
Kennesaw Mountain (18 June–3 July)	9
Peach Tree Creek (20 July)	54

---

[4] Weitz, "A Higher Duty," 117–55.

[5] This includes men killed, wounded, captured, or otherwise incapacitated, as well as lightly wounded. Some of the figures represent men who were wounded multiple times.

Atlanta (22 July)	37
Skirmishes around Atlanta (8–30 August)	39
Jonesboro (31 August–1 September)	23
Other engagements	25
Tennessee Campaign (October –January 1865)	
Decatur (28 October)	29
Franklin (31 November)	3
Second Murfreesboro (7 December)	5
Nashville (15–16 December)	26
Retreat (17 December– early January)	14
Carolinas Campaign (February–April 1865)	
Binnaker's Bridge (8 February)	7
Bentonville (19–21 March)	9

Table 5.
Losses from Desertion, Chronologically, By Campaign or Period of Service[6]

Recruitment and duty in Florida	35[7]	(May–September 1863)
Chattanooga Campaign	10	(October–November 1863)
Dalton encampment	23[8]	(December 1863–April, 1864)
Atlanta campaign	9	(May–July 1864)
Siege of Atlanta	7	(August–September 1864)
Tennessee Campaign	2	(October–December, 1864)

---

[6] Includes both men who deserted and returned or were recaptured, and men who deserted permanently.

[7] These figures are combined because part of the regiment served in Florida while the rest continued recruiting, and because, while dates of desertion are given in the compiled service records, they are not always specific about whether the man in question left service at Macon or at Quincy.

[8] Includes those known to have deserted and those who took leaves of absence from which they did not return.

As for the regiment's actual battlefield record, at Resaca, Nisbet's men fought bravely, but and they held the town more because of extreme enemy caution than because of their own martial prowess. At Peach Tree Creek, they attacked trenches, lost heavily, and did not make a dent in the Union line. At the Battle of Atlanta they were ambushed, and, whether they fled in panic, or merely became lost, they do not seem to have fought particularly well. There are no details of their roles at Jonesboro or Franklin, but the rout of their brigade at Second Murfreesboro must have been embarrassing.

What can explain this mediocre performance? Apart from inexperienced officers, which may have left the regiment somewhat stunted, there are other factors to consider.[9] First, Confederates in the Western Theater lost most of the battles. Peach Tree Creek, Atlanta, Jonesboro, Franklin, Second Murfreesboro, and Nashville were but a continuation of earlier reverses at Fort Donelson, Shiloh, Perryville, Murfreesboro, and Missionary Ridge. Second, Nisbet's men faced a tough and determined enemy. Federal soldiers in the Western Theater were self-confident, undaunted by setbacks or privations, and sure of victory. Like Lee's Confederates in Virginia, Western Theater Yankees had a record of steady victories. When the Atlanta Campaign began, they were veterans in the fullest sense. Is it surprising that the untested 66th Georgia could not do so?[10] Third, many of the men in the 66th Georgia were older than the average soldier. They could not march as quickly or deploy into battle as crisply as younger Confederates—or younger Federals, for

---

[9] Richard McMurry traces the more consistent victories of Lee's Army of Northern Virginia in part to its ability to attract and retain a greater number of army veterans and experienced men in regimental positions than did the Army of Tennessee (*Two Great Rebel Armies*, 87–105).

[10] Daniel, *Soldiering in the Army of Tennessee*, 20.

that matter. Already at a disadvantage in age and experience, their bodies were soon broken down by fighting an "unrelenting [campaign], marked by constant fighting, daily advances and retreats, [and] constant physical labor."[11] With so many lost from sickness and exhaustion, the regiment had too few men at Peach Tree Creek and Atlanta, and these few were probably too tired to fight effectively. Finally, there is the role of luck. What would have been the result had skirmishers been deployed on 20 July 1864, had Nisbet not been captured on 22 July, or had the regiment simply attacked elsewhere, none can say with certainty. Under any of these "what-if" scenarios, the outcomes of the battles probably would not have changed, but Nisbet and his men might have scored a few temporary, personal successes to boast of later.

What motivated the men of the 66th Georgia to keep fighting until April 1865? Perhaps a shared sense of hardship, religious revivals, army punishments, and "toughening up" on campaign were the key elements. Other motivations—such as a desire to protect home and family, a willingness to sacrifice for fellow soldiers, and a reluctance to dishonor the cause by deserting—might have also kept men in the ranks.[12]

When Civil War veteran William Fox studied regimental casualties in the postwar period, he concluded that unit pride explained why men gave their lives in bloody battles, time after time. "The private in the ranks," Fox wrote, "expects neither [glory] or [recognition]. His identity is merged in that of his regiment. To him the regiment and its name is everything."[13] The ties that bind soldiers to comrades, to armies, and to causes are best understood when examined at the level of the regiment. In

[11] Noe, *Reluctant Rebels,* 206, 210.
[12] Noe, *Reluctant Rebels,* 66–86, 155–69.
[13] William F. Fox, *Regimental Losses in the American Civil War, 1861–1865* (Albany NY: Brandon Printing Company, 1889) 575.

considering these fighting units, we not only give the "proper recognition of old commands," but also glean insights on how war affects individuals, whether officers or privates, volunteers or draftees, old or young, rich or poor.[14]

---

[14] Ibid.

Bibliography

Government Publications and Unpublished Manuscripts

Bowdoin, J. D. Letter, 23 June, 1864, Regimental Files, Georgia. Kennesaw Mountain National Battlefield Park, Archives.

Briggs Napier Collection. Middle Georgia Archives, Washington Memorial Library, Macon, Georgia.

Compiled Service Records, 66th Georgia Infantry. War Department Collection of Confederate Records, RG 109, National Archives and Records Administration, Washington, DC.

Davis family papers, Doug Fisher's private papers, Cardiff, Wales, UK.

Farrar, William T. Letter to Eliza Rains, 1 March 1864, Georgia Department of Archives and History, Atlanta, Georgia.

Georgia Confederate Pension Files

Index to the Letters Received by the Confederate Adjutant and Inspector General and by the Confederate Quartermaster General, 1861-1865. War Department Collection of Confederate Records, RG 109, National Archives and Records Administration, Washington, DC.

Inspection Reports and Related Records Received by the Inspection Branch in the Confederate Adjutant and Inspector General's Office, 1861-1865. War Department Collection of Confederate Records, RG 109, National Archives and Records Administration, Washington, DC.

James P. Crane Letters. Atlanta History Center, Atlanta, Georgia.

John M. Davis Letters. Georgia Department of Archives and History, Atlanta, Georgia.

LeConte, William Louis. "Events of My Life," unpublished memoir, William Louis LeConte private papers, Ellicott City, Maryland.

LeConte, William. Letter to mother, 28 February 1864. Georgia Department of Archives and History, Atlanta, Georgia.

Letters Received by the Confederate Adjutant General and Inspector General, 1861-1865. War Department Collection of Confederate Records, RG 109, National Archives and Records Administration, Washington, DC.

Letters Sent by the Confederate Adjutant General and Inspector General, 1861-1865. War Department Collection of Confederate Records, RG 109, National Archives and Records Administration, Washington, DC.

Letters Sent by the Confederate Secretary of War, 1861-1865. War Department Collection of Confederate Records, RG 109, National Archives and Records Administration, Washington, DC.

Napier, Briggs H. Reminiscences, Georgia Department of Archives and History, Atlanta, Georgia.

Napier-Blackman-Ross-Rose Family Collection. Middle Georgia Archives, Washington Memorial Library, Macon, Georgia.

Nisbet, James Cooper. Letter to Chickamauga-Chattanooga National Military Park, May 6, 1911, 66th Georgia Unit File, Chickamauga-Chattanooga National Military Park, Fort Oglethorpe, Georgia.

Robert G. Mitchell Letters. University of Georgia, Special Collections, Athens, Georgia.

Stevens, Clement H. Letter, April 10, 1864. South Caroliniana Collection, University of South Carolina, Columbia, South Carolina.

Telegrams Sent by the Confederate Secretary of War, 1861-1865. War Department Collection of Confederate Records, RG 109, National Archives and Records Administration, Washington, DC.

US Bureau of the Census. Eighth Census, 1860, Manuscript Returns of Free Inhabitants, Georgia.

US Bureau of the Census. Eighth Census, 1860, Manuscript Returns of Productions of Agriculture, Georgia.

US Bureau of the Census. Eighth Census, 1860, Manuscript Returns of Slaves, Georgia.

US Bureau of the Census. Ninth Census, 1870, Manuscript Returns of Inhabitants, Georgia.

US Bureau of the Census. Seventh Census, 1850, Manuscript Returns of Free Inhabitants, Georgia.

US War Department, compiler. *The War of the Rebellion: A Compilation of the Official Records of the Union and Confederate Armies.* 128 volumes. Washington, DC: Government Printing Office, 1880–1901.

William R. Hurst Papers. Kennesaw Mountain National Battlefield Park, Archives.

Newspapers and Periodicals
Athens *Southern Banner*
Athens *Southern Watchman*
Atlanta *Georgian and News*
Atlanta *Intelligencer*
Atlanta *Southern Confederacy*
Atlanta *Sunny South*
Atlanta *Weekly Constitution*
Atlanta *Weekly Sun*
Augusta Chronicle

Augusta *Daily Constitution*
Atlanta Journal
Columbus Ledger
Edgefield (SC) *Advertiser*
Leavenworth (KS) *Daily Times*
Macon Daily Telegraph
Macon Weekly Telegraph
Macon Telegraph
Milledgeville Confederate Union Weekly
Sumter Republican

Published primary sources

Allen, Randall, and Keith S. Bohannon, editors. *Campaigning with "Old Stonewall": Confederate Captain Ujanirtus Allen's Letters to His Wife.* Baton Rouge: Louisiana State University Press, 1998.

Andrews, W. H. *Footprints of a Regiment: A Recollection of the 1st Georgia Regulars, 1861-1865.* Atlanta: Longstreet Press, 1992.

Brief Biographies of the Members of the Constitutional Convention, July 11, 1877. Atlanta: Constitution Publishing Company, 1877.

Confederate Veteran. 40 volumes. Harrisburg PA: National Historical Society, 1893-1932.

Confederate Reminiscences and Letters, 1861-1865. 22 volumes. Atlanta: United Daughters of the Confederacy, 1995-2006.

Fox, William F. *Regimental Losses in the American Civil War, 1861-1865.* Albany NY: Brandon Printing Company, 1889.

Hughes, Nathan, editor. *The Civil War Memoirs of P. D. Stephenson,* Conway: University of Central Arkansas Press, 1995.

Johnston, Robert U., and Clarence C. Buell, editors. *Battles and Leaders of the Civil War,* 4 volumes. New York: Century Press, 1887.

Johnston, Joseph E. *A Narrative of Military Operations.* New York: D. Appleton and Co., 1874.

Nisbet, James Cooper. *Four Years on the Firing Line.* Chattanooga: Imperial Press, 1911.

Reminiscences of Confederate Soldiers and Stories of the War. 14 volumes. United Daughters of the Confederacy, 1940.

Southern Historical Society Papers. Wilmington NC: Broadfoot Publishing Company, 1990-1992.

Thomas, Henry W. *History of The Doles-Cook Brigade, Army of Northern Virginia, C.S.A.* Atlanta: Franklin Printing & Publishing Co., 1903.

Watkins, Sam. *Company Aytch: A Sideshow Of the Big Show.* New York: Collier Books, 1962.

Articles

Billings, Elden E. "The Civil War and Conscription," *Current History* 54/322 (June 1968): 333-38, 366.

Bohannon, Keith. "Cadets, Drillmasters, Draft Dodgers, and Soldiers: The Georgia Military Institute During the Civil War," *The Georgia Historical Quarterly* 79/1 (Spring 1995): 5-29.

Carlson, David. "The 'Loanly Runagee': Draft Evaders in Confederate South Georgia," *Georgia Historical Quarterly* 84/4 (Winter 2000): 589-615.

Maslowski, Pete. "A Study of Morale in Civil War Soldiers," *Military Affairs* 34/4 (December 1970): 122-26.

McMurry, Richard M. "Confederate Morale in the Atlanta Campaign of 1864," *Georgia Historical Quarterly* 54/2 (Summer 1970): 226-43.

———. "The Atlanta Campaign of 1864: A New Look," *Civil War History* 22/1 (March 1976): 5-15.

McNeill, William J. "A Survey of Confederate Soldier Morale During Sherman's Campaign through Georgia and the Carolinas," *The Georgia Historical Quarterly* 55/1 (Spring 1971): 1–25.

O'Kelley, Harold. "The Story of Bill Truelove," *North Georgia Journal* (Winter 1992): 59–60.

Sacher, John. "The Loyal Draft Dodger?: A Reexamination of Confederate Substitution," *Civil War History* 57/2 (June 2011): 153-78.

Shaw, William L. "The Confederate Conscription and Exemption Acts," *American Journal of Legal History* 6/4 (October 1962): 368-405.

Sheehan-Dean, Aaron. "Justice Has Something to Do with It: Class Relations and the Confederate Army," *Virginia Magazine of History and Biography* 113/4 (2005): 340-77.

Smith, David G. "Georgians Seem to Suffer More Than Any Troops in the Service": A Profile of Two Companies of Madison County Confederates," *Georgia Historical Quarterly* 79/1 (Spring 1995): 169-91.

Starr, Stephen Z. "The Grand Old Regiment," *Wisconsin Magazine of History* 48/1 (Autumn 1964): 21-31.

"Telamon C. S. Cuyler," *History Notes* 3/ 1 (Spring 2005): 2-3.

Vaughan, David W. "Georgians In Gray, Part II: A Photographic Look at the Empire State's Confederate Soldiers," *Georgia Historical Quarterly* 89/2 (Summer 2005): 213–41.

Dissertations, Theses, and Forthcoming Publications

Cone, Daniel. "Last to Join the Fight: the Sixty-sixth Georgia Infantry."
Masters thesis, University of West Georgia, 2012.

Weitz, Mark Alan. "A Higher Duty: Desertion among Georgia Troops during
the Civil War." Ph.D. dissertation. Arizona State University, 1998.

McMurry, Richard M. "The Atlanta Campaign: December 23, 1864 to July,
18, 1864." Ph.D. dissertation, Emory University, 1967.

Secondary Sources

Avery, Isaac W. *The History of the State of Georgia from 1850 to 1881.* New
York: Brown & Derby Publishers, 1881.

Ballard, Michael B. *Vicksburg: The Campaign that Opened the Mississippi.*
Chapel Hill: University of North Carolina Press, 2004.

Brown, Russell K. *To the Manner Born: The Life of General William H. T.
Walker.* Macon GA: Mercer University Press, 2005.

Bryan, T. Conn. *Confederate Georgia.* Athens: University of Georgia Press,
1953.

Castel, Albert. *Decision in the West: The Atlanta Campaign of 1864.* Lawrence:
University Press of Kansas, 1992.

Cozzens, Peter. *The Shipwreck of Their Hopes: The Battles for Chattanooga.*
Chicago: University of Illinois Press, 1994.

Crute, Joseph H., Jr. *Units of the Confederate Army.* Midlothian VA: Derwent
Books, 1987.

Daniel, Larry J. *Soldiering in the Army of the Tennessee.* Chapel Hill: University
of North Carolina Press, 1991.

Davis, Stephen. *Atlanta Will Fall: Sherman, Joe Johnston, and the Heavy Yankee
Battalions.* Wilmington DE: Scholarly Resources Books, 2001.

Ecelbarger, Gary. *The Day Dixie Died: The Battle of Atlanta.* New York:
Thomas Dunne Books, 2010.

Fowler, John D. *Mountaineers in Gray: The Nineteenth Tennessee Volunteer
Infantry, C.S.A.* Knoxville: University of Tennessee Press, 2004.

Gallagher, Gary W. *The Confederate War.* Cambridge: Harvard University
Press, 1999.

———, editor. *The Shenandoah Valley Campaign of 1862.* Chapel Hill:
University of North Carolina Press, 2003.

Glatthaar, Joseph T. *General Lee's Army: From Victory to Collapse.* New York:
Simon and Schuster, 2008.

Haggerty, Edward J. *Collis' Zouaves: The 114th Pennsylvania Volunteers in the
Civil War.* Baton Rouge: Louisiana State University Press, 1997.

Haughton, Andrew. *Training, Tactics and Leadership in the Confederate Army of Tennessee: Seeds of Failure*. London: Frank Cass Publishers, 2000.

Henderson, Lillian, editor. *Roster of the Confederate Soldiers of Georgia, 1861-1865*. Hapeville GA: Longino & Porter, 1964.

Hewitt, Janet B. *Georgia's Confederate Soldiers, 1861-1865*, 4 volumes. Wilmington NC: Broadfoot Publishing Co., 1998.

Hewitt, Lawrence Lee, and Arthur W. Bergeron, Jr., editors. *Confederate Generals in the Western Theater, Vol. I: Classic Essays on America's Civil War*. Knoxville: University of Tennessee Press, 2010.

Jenkins, Sr., Robert D. *The Battle of Peach Tree Creek: Hood's First Sortie*. Macon GA: Mercer University Press, 2014.

Kownslar, Allan O., editor. *Teaching American History: The Quest for Relevancy*. National Council for the Social Studies, 1974.

Martin, George Winston. *"I Will Give Them One More Shot": Ramsey's 1st Georgia Volunteers*. Macon GA.: Mercer University Press, 2010.

McMurry, Richard M. *Two Great Rebel Armies: An Essay in Confederate Military History*. Chapel Hill: University of North Carolina Press, 1988.

_____. *Atlanta, 1864: Last Chance for the Confederacy*. Lincoln: University of Nebraska Press, 2000.

Moore, Albert Burton. *Conscription and Conflict in the Confederacy*. New York: The Macmillan Co., 1924.

Noe, Kenneth W. *Reluctant Rebels: The Confederates Who Joined the Army after 1861*. Chapel Hill: University of North Carolina Press, 2010.

Parks, Joseph Howard. *Joseph E. Brown of Georgia*. Baton Rouge: Louisiana State University Press, 1976.

Sams, Anita B. *Wayfarers in Walton: A History of Walton County, Georgia, 1818-1967*. Monroe, GA: Walton Press, Inc., 1967.

Sarris, Jonathan Dean. *A Separate Civil War: Communities in Conflict in the Mountain South*. Charlottesville: University of Virginia Press, 2006.

Savas, Theodore P., editor. *The Campaign for Atlanta and Sherman's March to the Sea: Essays on the American Civil War in Georgia, 1864*. 2 volumes. Campbell CA.: Savas Woodbury Publishers, 1994.

Scaife, William R. *The Campaign for Atlanta*. Cartersville GA: Scaife Publications, 1993.

———, and William Harris Bragg. *Joe Brown's Pets: The Georgia Militia, 1862-1865*. Macon: Mercer University Press, 2004.

Sword, Wiley. *Embrace an Angry Wind: The Confederacy's Last Hurrah—Spring Hill, Franklin and Nashville*. New York: Harper Collins, 1992.

Trudeau, Noah Anne. *Gettysburg: A Testing of Courage*. New York: Harper Collins Publishers, 2001.

Weitz, Mark Alan. *A Higher Duty: Desertion among Georgia Troops during the Civil War*. Lincoln: University of Nebraska Press, 2000.

Wetherington, Mark V. *Plain Folks' Fight: The Civil War & Reconstruction in Piney Woods Georgia*. Chapel Hill: University of North Carolina Press, 2005.

Wiggins, Dr. David R. *Remembering Georgia's Confederates*. Charleston, SC, Chicago, IL, Portsmouth, NH, and San Francisco, CA: Altamira Press, 2005.

Wiley, Bell I. *The Life of Johnny Reb: The Common Soldier of the Confederacy*. Baton Rouge: Louisiana State University Press, 1943.

Williams, David, Teresa Crisp Williams, and David Carlson. *Plain Folk in a Rich Man's War: Class and Dissent in Confederate Georgia*. Gainesville: University Press of Florida, 2002.

Williams, David. *Rich Man's War: Class, Caste, and Confederate Defeat in the Lower Chattahoochee River Valley*. Athens: University of Georgia Press, 1998.

Woodworth, Steven. *Six Armies in Tennessee: The Chickamauga and Chattanooga Campaign*. Lincoln: University of Nebraska Press, 1998.

_____. *Nothing But Victory: The Army of the Tennessee, 1861-1865*. New York: Vintage Books, 2005.

_____. *Decision in the Heartland: The Civil War in the West*. Westport CT: Praeger, 2008.

Blogs and Internet Resources

"Biography of Captain Briggs H. Napier," http://www.armoryguards.org/briggs_napier.htm.

Confederate Pension Applications, 1879-1960, Civil War Records, www.ancestry.com.

"Elizabeth Maxey Berrie Hull Tucker," www.woodenshipsironmen.com/Articles/Berry.htm

"John Morgan Davis – Family Tree," http://hawkofgeorgia.com/webtrees/individual.php?pid=I263&ged=2006113 0v.ged.

"Report of Deaths at Augusta, Georgia," www.confederatevets.com/documents.

"Soldiers Cemetery in Eastern Cemetery, Quincy, Florida," http://pone.com/ts/EasternCemetery001.htm.

TOCWOC—A Civil War Blog, www.brettschulte.net/CWBLOG.

Index

Hurst, Pvt. William R.: and
 Atlanta Campaign, 123-125,
 127; at Camp Cobb, 84-85;
 death, 141; morale, 99, 103-
 104; on conditions in 66th
 Georgia, 123, 134-135, on
 personal religion, 106-107
Jackson, Brig. Gen. Henry R.: 148,
 155-158
Jackson, Lt. Gen. Thomas J.
 "Stonewall": 29, 33, 47, 115,
 175
Johnson's Island (Prisoner-of-war
 camp), Oh.: 166-167
Johnston, Gen. Joseph E.: and
 cautious strategy in Atlanta
 Campaign, 113-122;
 establishes officer examination
 boards, 111; opposes Sherman
 in Carolinas, 162-164;
 punishes deserters, 109;
 relieved by Davis, 125-126;
 retreats across Chattahoochee
 River, 124-125; soldiers'
 reaction to relief, 126-128,
 175; takes command at
 Dalton, 100-102
Jonesboro, Ga., Battle of: 146,
 147, 189-190
Jordan, Capt. Columbus M.: 69
Kennesaw Mountain, Ga., Battle
 of: 121-124, 188
Kennon, Emma Jane: 145-146
Langston, Capt. Thomas L.: 69,
 142, 173
LeConte, Adj. William: 42-43,
 100, 113, 127, 139
Lee, General Robert E.: 7, 29, 33,
 39, 88, 175
Leverett, Thomas: 41-42, 76

Lumpkin County, Ga: 25-26
Macon, Ga.: 24, 27, 32-34, 43-44,
 80, 84, 88, 101-102, 146, 149,
 164, 168
Macon Daily Telegraph
 (newspaper): 5. 15, 28, 174
Madison County, Ga.: 52
Manassas, Va., First Battle of (First
 Bull Run): 17-18, 29, 48
McPherson, Maj. Gen. James B.:
 117-120, 128-129, 135, 137,
 140
Mercer, Col. John T.: 29-32, 34-
 35, 38-39
Milledgeville, Ga.: 4, 29
Milledgeville Confederate Union
 (newspaper): 4, 8, 9, 14-15
Mississippi: 6, 44-45, 88, 113
Missionary Ridge, Tn., Battle of:
 93-99, 107, 157
Moody, Ascon Q.: 48, 63, 163
Murfreesboro, Tn., First Battle of:
 7, 190
Murfreesboro, Tn., Second Battle
 of: 154-156, 189-190
Napier, Lt. Briggs H.: attempts to
 return to active service, 44-46;
 background and early-war
 illness, 42-44; marries after
 war, 172-173; on personal
 morale, 102; on state of
 regiment before Peach Tree
 Creek, 129, 134; personal and
 parental wealth of 65-66, 69;
 reacts to relief of Johnston,
 127; suffers wound and
 amputation, 132, 141-142;
 visits Nisbet in Macon, 168
Nashville, Tn.: 151, 153-154, 168

Schofield, Maj. Gen. John M.:
128, 151-153
Seddon, Confed. Sec. of War
James: 35-36, 39, 83, 111
Sherman, Maj. Gen. William T.:
and cautious strategy in Atlanta
Campaign, 120-122; at Dalton
and Resaca, Battles of, 115-
118; at Tunnel Hill, Tn.,
Battle of, 94-95; begins
"March to the Sea," 151;
captures Atlanta, 146; chases
Hood into Alabama, 148-150;
crosses Chattahoochee River,
124; marches through the
Carolinas, 162-163; surrounds
Atlanta, 128
Sixty-sixth (66th) Georgia Infantry:
and officer examination boards
in, 111-112; and relations to
Confederate home front, 104-
106, 151, 160; and religion in,
106-108; as envisioned by
Nisbet, 34-37; as one of last
Confederate units raised in
Georgia, 22, 26-27;
assessments of combat
performance, 119-120, 131,
139-140, 190-191; at Camp
Cobb, 84-87, 89; at Camp
Cooper, 80-84; at
Chickamauga Station, 96-97;
at Dalton winter camp, 100-
114; casualties, accidental, 87;
casualties, battle, 87, 98, 118-
120, 122, 131-134, 141, 150-
151, 156-157, 186-189;
casualties, desertions, 63, 66,
81-82, 87, 98-100, 109, 123,
134, 146, 158, 186-189

casualties, other, 123-124,
143-144; casualties, sickness,
82, 87, 98, 123, 134-135, 143,
186-187; Company A of, 53,
67, 81, 142; Company B of,
53, 67, 142; Company C of,
53, 55, 67, 74, 142; Company
D of, 51-53, 67, 74, 142;
Company E of, 53, 67, 74;
Company F of, 53, 55, 67;
Company G of, 67, 142;
Company H of, 53, 67, 81,
142; Company I of, 67;
Company K of, 67, 142;
consolidated into 1st Georgia
Battalion, 164; consolidated
with 1st Georgia Infantry, 148-
149; criticisms of, 110-111,
143-144; deaths of veterans in
immediate aftermath of war,
168-169; demographics–age
ranges of soldiers in, 3, 53-55,
98, 143-144, 149, 159-161,
164-165; demographics–as
compared to other Confederate
soldiers, 72-73, 79;
demographics–carpenters in,
61-62; demographics–clerks in,
62; demographics–conscripts
in, 73, 76-77, 158-161;
demographics–counties of
origin, 52-53, 98, 159-161,
164-165, 193-195;
demographics–deserters and
absentees, 63, 66, 81-82, 98-
100, 109, 143-144, 149, 158-
161, 188; demographics–
farmers in, 57-59;
demographics–farm acreage,
58-59, 78, 99; demographics–

sample group of, 207-220;
slave-owners and slave-owning
families represented in, 221-
225; states of morale, 137-138,
162; summary of attrition
suffered by, 186-189; summary
of demographics of soldiers in,
184; supplies sent to, 90, 101-
102; transferred to South
Carolina, 161-162; veterans in,
38-50 , 185; volunteer bounty
for, 4, 73-74, 76
Snake Creek Gap, Ga., 116-117,
119-120
South Carolina: 6, 19, 88
Spring Hill, Tn., Affair at: 151-
152
Stevens, Gen. Clement H.:
replaces Nisbet as brigade
commander, 109-110;
criticizes 66th Georgia, 110-
111; and officer examination
boards, 111-112; regrets relief
of Johnston, 125-126; death
of, 132, 141, 148
Summers, Lt. A. Jackson: 65, 68-
69
Tennessee: 10-11, 19, 23, 45, 149,
151, 161
Tennessee River: 150-151
Tennessee Campaign: 149-158,
161, 189
Thomas, Maj. Gen. George H.:
128, 135, 151, 156-157
Thornton, Capt. Jesse: 47-49, 69,
111-112
Tunnel Hill, Ga.., Skirmish of:
112-113
Tunnel Hill, Tn., Battle of: 94-95

Union Army (United States
Army): 6-8
Union Army (United States
Army), military units: 14th
Michigan Infantry, 145; 14th
Ohio Light Artillery, 137-138;
27th Ohio Infantry, 138-139;
39th Ohio Infantry, 138-139;
128th Ohio Infantry, 166-167;
Army of the Cumberland: 7,
88-89, 95-96, 128; Army of
the Ohio: 128; Army of the
Potomac: 7; Army of the
Tennessee: 117-120, 128-129,
135, 137-140
Vicksburg, Ms., Siege of: 7, 8, 75,
88, 99-100
Virginia: 7, 17, 18, 29, 45, 46,
150, 175-176
Walker, Gen. William H. T.: 90,
140
War Department, Confederate:
33-36, 76, 80, 83, 88
War weariness, North, 6-8, 116
Weaver, Commissary Sgt. Graves
H.: 171, 179
Weaver, Pvt. William M.: 41-42,
69
Western Theater: 8, 44-45, 175,
190
Wheeler, Maj. Gen. Joseph: 129
Williams, Jr., William T.: 48-49
Williamson, Capt. Charles J.: 43,
69, 132, 169, 171
Wilson, Gen. Claudius: 90-91,
109